A Literary Holiday Cookbook

By the same author

A Literary Tea Party

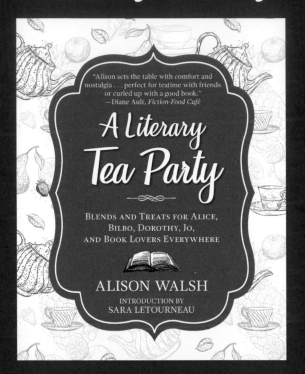

A Literary Holiday Cookbook

Festive Meals for the Snow Queen, Gandalf, Sherlock, Scrooge, and Book Lovers Everywhere

Alison Walsh

Foreword by Haley Stewart

Skyhorse Publishing

Skyhorse Publishing books may be purchased in bulk at special discounts for sales promotion, corporate gifts, fund-raising, or educational purposes. Special editions can also be created to specifications. For details, contact the Special Sales Department, Skyhorse Publishing, 307 West 36th Street, 11th Floor, New York, NY 10018 or info@skyhorsepublishing.com.

Skyhorse® and Skyhorse Publishing® are registered trademarks of Skyhorse Publishing, Inc.®, a Delaware corporation.

Visit our website at www.skyhorsepublishing.com.

10 9 8 7 6 5 4 3

Library of Congress Cataloging-in Publication Data is available on file.

Cover design by Erin Seaward-Hiatt and Daniel Brount
Cover illustration from Shutterstock
Photographs by Alison Walsh

Print ISBN: 978-1-5107-5496-6
Ebook ISBN: 978-1-5107-6170-4

Printed in China

For the Little Miss, a true hobbit at heart

contents

Foreword   xi

Introduction   1

Tips, Tricks, and Substitutions   5

CHRISTMAS   8

A Christmas Carol: A Dickensian Christmastide   11
    Applesauce   13
    Onion and Sage Roasted Goose   15
    Chocolate Profiterole Christmas Puddings 17
    Duchess Potatoes   21

The Chronicles of Narnia: Food for the Long Winter   23
    Diggory's Apple Bites   25
    Turkey from Aslan's Table   27
    Turkish Delight   29
    Mrs. Beaver's Potatoes   33

Little Women: Christmas with the March Family   35
    Rustic Whole Wheat Bread   37
    Turkey Roulade   39
    Baked Apples   43
    Jo's Gingerbread   44

"The Nutcracker and the Mouse King": Feast of the Sugar Plum Fairy   47
    Garlic Rosemary Toasted Almonds   49
    Pesto and Bacon Puff Pastry Christmas Tree   51
    Mouse King Cheese Bites   55
    Sugar Plums   57

White Fang: Hearty Wilderness Fare   59
    Arctic Trail Coffee Muffins   61

Seared Salmon with Lemon Dill Butter 63
White Whiskey Baked Beans with Bacon 65
S'mores Baked Alaska 67

THANKSGIVING 70

The Hobbit: **A Long-Expected Thanksgiving** 73
Beorn's Honey Nut Banana Bread 75
Melton Mowbray: Mini Pork Pies 77
Hobbit Door Giant Chocolate Chip Cookie 79
Bag End Orchard Salad 83

The Little House books: Holiday on the Homestead 85
Skillet Cornbread with Homemade Butter 87
Simple Roasted Sweet Potatoes 89
Venison Pot Roast 91
Maple Candy 93

Redwall: An Autumnal Abbey Feast 95
Loamhedge Nutbread 97
Leek and Potato Soup with Parsnip and Garlic 99
Deeper 'n Ever Turnip 'n Tater 'n Beetroot Pie 101
Damson Plum and Pear Crumbles with Meadowcream and Mint 103

"The Legend of Sleepy Hollow": Dinner at the Van Tassel Mansion 107
Apple Cider Crullers 109
Brown Sugar Glazed Turkey 111
Smashed Pumpkin Soup 113
Maple Walnut Apple Pie 115

Winnie-the-Pooh: **A Hundred Acre Celebration** 119
Haycorns 121
Cottleston Pie 123
Rabbit's Autumn Harvest Salad 125
Pooh's Honey Lemon Cookies 127

HALLOWEEN 128

Dracula: A Few Quick Bites   **131**
Renfield's Spider Chips and Salsa   133
Robber "Stakes"   135
Dracula's Dinner Rolls   137
Monstrous Moon Pies   139

Complete Tales & Poems by Edgar Allan Poe:
Once upon a Midnight Party   **143**
Deviled Raven Eggs   145
Coffin Pizza Pockets   147
Moon Phase Fries   149
Masque of the Red Death Skeleton Cookies   151

Sherlock Holmes: Snacks for Sleuths   **153**
Blood Orange Scones   155
Roasted Tomato Deviled Scotch Eggs   157
Sherlock's Steak Sandwiches   161
London Fog Mystery Cookies   163

The Wonderful Wizard of Oz: A Technicolor Banquet   **167**
Emerald City Popcorn   169
Pizza Pinwheel Cyclones   171
Melted Witch Chips and Guacamole   173
Pumpkin Winged Monkey Bread   175

NEW YEAR 176

Alice's Adventures in Wonderland: A Mad New Year's Party   **179**
Card Suit Cheese Bites   181
The Queen of Hearts's Tomato Tart   183
Herbed Mushroom Puffs   187
Eat Me Cakes   189

The Phantom of the Opera: A New Year's Masquerade   **193**
Devils on Horseback: Bacon-Wrapped Dates   195

Apple Rose Tartlets 197

Savory Strawberry Éclairs 199

Chocolate Strawberry Opera Cake 203

"The Snow Queen": Winter Wonderland Dainties 207

Fried Snowballs 209

Savory Snowflake Bread 211

Gerda's Cherry Bites 215

Mirror Shard Mini Ice Cream Cakes 217

FESTIVE SIPS 219

Drink Me Punch 221

Jo March's Hot Cocoa Mix 223

The Phantom's Rose 225

Poe's Nevermore Cocktail 227

Pumpkin Cider 229

The White Witch's White Chocolate Chai Latte 231

Wicked Witch Punch 233

DELECTABLE GIFTS TO SUIT THE SEASON 235

Candied Walnuts 236

Spiced Pine Nuts 236

Flavored Butter 237

Fruit Curd 238

Homemade Marshmallows 239

Honeycomb Candy 240

Infused Honey 241

Infused Sugar 243

Pesto (Basil and Sun-Dried Tomato) 244

Syrups (Blueberry, Pumpkin, and Strawberry) 246

References 249

Conversion Charts 251

Index 253

Foreword

In times of crisis, two things never fail to bring consolation: good books and good food. At the time of this writing, during a global pandemic, this has never been more true. While deprived of "normal" life, people in quarantine are coping by baking and reaching for long-beloved comfort reads. In my home, my husband bakes fresh sourdough bread daily that we eat with jam in the afternoon while I read aloud our favorite books to my four children. This little quotidian tradition is a delicious glimmer of beauty and goodness during a time of suffering.

Wonderful food and good stories comfort us. They remind us to be hopeful when our lives seem dark. And sharing meals and stories around a table reminds us that we are human beings who are made to feast. We are wired for festivity just as we are wired for story. Perhaps this is why stories about feasting are forever imprinted on our hearts.

The classic tales that hold our hearts are stories we inhabit. We see ourselves attending a feast at Redwall Abbey, being offered a taste of Turkish delight by a mysterious queen, or smelling the intoxicating scent of the March family's Christmas breakfast being carried over snowy lanes to offer to the poor Hummels. Our mouths water each time we reread these familiar passages, but, alas, the feasts are only in our imaginations—until now.

Alison Walsh offers us the opportunity to bring the feasts of literary classics to our own homes! The fantasies of joining the Cratchits at their Christmas table, sampling Ma Ingalls's maple candy, or sharing Cottleston pie with Winnie-the-Pooh are fantasies no longer. Each of these authentic recipes is meticulously informed by the text inspiring it. Whether you're ready to put on an apron or brew a cup of tea and cozy up with some literary recipes, you will be delighted.

This lovely book offers you the chance to rediscover classic tales and bring them to life in your kitchen. So join your friends within the pages of beloved books with friends around your table! No matter what storms rage outside, it is always the right time to celebrate the gift of a good book and a tasty meal—let this beautiful cookbook be your guide.

—Haley Stewart, podcaster, speaker, and author of
The Grace of Enough and *The Literary Medicine Cabinet*

Introduction

Dear Reader,

People are often surprised to hear that I haven't always loved cooking. In fact, I did my fair share of whining whenever I needed to help make dinner as a kid. It wasn't until I bought my first cookbook in college that I realized food could be a creative outlet. After that, it didn't take long for me to fall hopelessly in love.

But I have *always* loved books.

As a toddler I would pull out the two biggest books we had—the dictionary and the Bible—and patiently scan page after page, not understanding a word yet completely engrossed. When I really learned to read, I devoured books insatiably. Looking back, it seems inevitable that I began to incorporate fiction into my food, first with my literary food blog, *Alison's Wonderland Recipes*, then with cookbooks.

When I sat down to write *A Literary Holiday Cookbook*, I wanted to create a cookbook both food lovers and fiction lovers could enjoy. It was important to me that this book welcome readers of all culinary skill levels. Naturally, I wanted to push the boundaries of my own culinary skills and creativity, but not at the expense of ease of use. I firmly believe you shouldn't have to know a ball whisk from a fish spatula to enjoy food from your favorite literature.

I feel the same way about holiday food. After all, holidays were created to be celebrations, and that's how they should feel. You shouldn't have to be utterly intimidated by roasting a turkey or baking an elegant dessert. It should be fun, and you should be able to look at the recipe and think, *I can do this!*

That's why, within these pages, you'll find recipes written for a variety of skill levels. The Mouse King Cheese Bites from "The Nutcracker" (page 55) are just right for those looking for a fun, festive, ultra-easy dish. The Loamhedge Nutbread from *Redwall* (page 97) lets you dip your toes into breadmaking, while the Rustic Whole Wheat Bread from *Little Women* (page 37) lets you dive in deep. For those familiar with cake-making and hungry for a challenge, the Chocolate Strawberry Opera Cake from *The Phantom of the Opera* (page 203) is four recipes in one—joconde sponge, homemade strawberry syrup, almond buttercream, and ganache.

Yet even the challenging recipes are designed to still feel approachable for anyone looking to learn a new skill. Each recipe is broken down into clear, digestible steps, with techniques and terms clarified for anyone who might be unfamiliar. The whole wheat bread mentioned earlier gives detailed instructions for shaping your loaf, and even the opera cake is broken down into easy steps. The roasted turkey and goose recipes don't involve brining, trussing, or elaborate stuffing. Instead, I went for glazes, spice rubs, and aromatics—easy ways to elevate such dishes from plain to elegant.

In short, no matter who you are or whether you know how to chiffonade basil, there is a place for you at this holiday table. Take a seat next to Jo March and Aslan, let Gandalf pour you a drink, and join all the beasts of Redwall in a festive song. The holidays are here!

—Alison

Hot Cocoa

1. Using a microwave-safe mug, heat
1 cup milk in a microwave on high
for 1½ minutes, stirring halfway through.
2. When milk is steaming, stir in ¼ cup
cocoa mix.
3. Enjoy!

* contains 4 servings

Jo March's Hot Cocoa Mix, page 223

in my usual absurd way. The things were just what
etter for being made instead of bought. Beth's ne
and ... of hard gingerbread will be a
u for the nice flannels you sent, Marmee, and
r he marked. Thank you all, heaps and heap
minds me that I'm getting rich in t t ti , on
aer gave me a fine Shakespeare. It s one he values
mired it, set up in the place of h or with his Ger-
r, and Milton, so you may imagi e how I felt when
hout its cover, and sh ved me m own name in it,
h Bhaer."

wish a library. Here I gif you one, for between these
many books in one. Read him well, and he will help
of character in this book will help you to read it in
ith your pen."

ll as I could, and talk now about "my library," as

Tips, Tricks, and Substitutions

Every chef needs a few good shortcuts up their sleeve to save the day when they're short on time or don't have a special ingredient on hand. Here are my favorite kitchen tips and tricks:

- **DIY Double Boiler.** If you don't have a double boiler, just place a regular ceramic bowl over a saucepan filled with boiling water. Make sure the water level is low enough that the bottom of the bowl doesn't touch the top of the water.
- **Quick Buttermilk Substitute.** Mix 1 cup milk with 1 tablespoon lemon juice and allow to sit for 5 minutes.
- **Room-Temperature Eggs.** If a recipe calls for room-temperature eggs and you forgot to let them sit out, submerge the eggs in very warm water for 10 minutes, then use as per normal.
- **Instant Softened Butter.** Sometimes I don't have the time to soften butter, or my winter kitchen isn't warm enough for it to soften when left to sit out. To instantly soften butter, place it between two sheets of wax paper and roll it to about ¼-inch thickness with a rolling pin. Quickly peel off the paper and use as per normal.
- **Liquid vs. Gel Food Coloring.** Some of the recipes in this book call for gel food coloring, while some call for standard liquid coloring. Gel is more condensed and therefore introduces less water into the recipe, while achieving a more intense color. I've specified the use of gel coloring in recipes where it's recommended, but if it's an emergency and you need to substitute it, the conversion is easy: use 2 to 3 drops of liquid for every drop of gel.
- **Quick Dough Cleanup.** Many cookie recipes call for flouring a surface (usually a countertop) and rolling out dough. If quick cleanup is a priority, roll out your dough on a large floured cutting board, which can be quickly rinsed off or thrown in the dishwasher when finished.
- **Sticky Measuring Spoons.** Accurately measuring sticky liquid ingredients like honey and syrup can be a pain—some of it always manages to stick to the spoon! For some recipes, you can avoid this by coating the spoon in a thin layer of cooking spray before adding in your ingredient, as long as fats such as butter or eggs will be added in the same step or have already been added. For example, if you are making muffins that call for honey, you can spray the spoon with cooking spray if you're adding your fats in

the same step or if they've already been mixed in. For recipes that are very finicky about the addition of fats (such as meringues), do not use this trick as it can add too much fat to the recipe.

- **Swapping Salted and Unsalted Butter.** Some recipes call for unsalted butter but still include salt in the list of ingredients. This is to allow for exact measurements and a more consistent result. However, if you are in a bind and find you don't have the right butter, don't panic. There is approximately 1/4 teaspoon salt in every 1/2 cup salted butter, so use this ratio to adjust your recipe in an emergency. Although it's not recommended for regular use, it shouldn't make a huge difference. This cannot be done for recipes that call for no salt at all, such as some pie crusts.

Christmas

Merry Christmas
Good Cheer

LITTLE WOMEN
LOUISA MAY ALCOTT
SIGNATURE EDITIONS

Getting Ahead of Santa Claus

Some of the core scenes in works of classic literature center on the family Christmas dinner table. Who can forget the humble but generous Christmas dinner of the March family in *Little Women* or that of the Crachits in *A Christmas Carol*? There is an intimacy to these scenes, as though the author is welcoming us to be part of the family. However, these moments of plenty also play a deeper role by providing a contrast to poverty. In *Little Women*, the poverty is material—the Marchs make sacrifices in order to have a celebratory Christmas breakfast, but then choose to give their food away to the Hummels, a family in greater need. In *A Christmas Carol*, Scrooge stares through the Cratchits' window and sees the generosity and warmth within, signified by the mutual effort of each family member to create the meal on the table. Meanwhile Scrooge himself is shut out in the cold alone, starving for the love he sees inside.

These classic works remind us that, while Christmas can be a time of material abundance, the true gift of the season is generous love, challenging us to make Scrooge's pledge our own:

> "I will honour Christmas in my heart, and try to keep it all the year.
> I will live in the Past, the Present, and the Future. The Spirits of all
> Three shall strive within me. I will not shut out the lessons that they
> teach."
>
> —Scrooge, *A Christmas Carol*, Charles Dickens

A Dickensian Christmastide

A Christmas Carol

By Charles Dickens

"God bless us, every one!"

Menu
Applesauce, 13
Onion and Sage Roasted Goose, 15
Chocolate Profiterole Christmas Puddings, 17
Duchess Potatoes, 21

Applesauce

Makes 6 cups

*"Mrs. Cratchit made the gravy (ready beforehand in a little saucepan)
hissing hot; Master Peter mashed the potatoes with incredible vigour;
Miss Belinda sweetened up the apple-sauce."*

One of the wonderful things about homemade applesauce is that you can customize the texture to your preference—whether you like your sauce satiny-smooth, chunky, or somewhere in between. It's also fun to play with aromatics. This recipe uses cinnamon, ginger, and lemon, but you can experiment with vanilla bean pods, whole cloves, nutmeg, orange peel, and more!

INGREDIENTS

3 lb. McIntosh apples
3 lb. Fuji apples
½ cup brown sugar, packed
¾ cup apple cider
1½ tablespoons fresh lemon juice
2 (1" x 2") strips lemon peel
2 cinnamon sticks
1 ounce fresh ginger, peeled and cut into 3 pieces
¼ teaspoon salt

INSTRUCTIONS

1 Peel and core the apples. Cut them into eighths and add to a large pot. Add all remaining ingredients and stir briefly to combine.

2 Place pot over medium heat and cover, cooking for 25 minutes, stirring occasionally. The McIntosh apples will mostly break down, and the Fujis will be mostly whole but very soft. Remove from heat. Remove and discard aromatics (lemon peel, cinnamon sticks, and ginger pieces). For a coarse texture, mash the apples in the pot with a potato masher or using the bottom of a heavy glass cup until desired consistency is reached. For a smooth texture, blend in a blender.

3 Transfer to an airtight container and chill in the refrigerator.

Serve at a Dickensian Christmas party!

Onion and Sage Roasted Goose

Makes 1 (10-lb.) goose

"And now two smaller Cratchits, boy and girl, came tearing in, screaming that outside the baker's they had smelt the goose, and known it for their own; and basking in luxurious thoughts of sage and onion, these young Cratchits danced about the table ..."

Goose was the star of the Cratchit family's Christmas dinner, and it can be for your family, too! The key to the perfect goose is managing the fat content. You don't want your goose sitting in inches of fat as it cooks, nor do you want to brine ahead of time, since geese aren't lean birds. The secret? Place the bird on a wire rack over a large baking sheet (rather than in a roasting pan) and siphon out the fat from the pan with a baster if it gets close to overflowing.

INGREDIENTS

1 (10-lb.) goose, neck and giblets removed
1½ tablespoons kosher salt, divided
½ teaspoon black pepper
2 tablespoons olive oil
1 teaspoon onion powder
2 large sage leaves, minced
1 yellow onion, quartered
2 large sprigs fresh sage
4 cloves garlic, peeled and crushed
1.5 ounces fresh ginger, peeled

Special Tools
13" x 18" baking sheet

INSTRUCTIONS

1 Pat the goose dry with a paper towel and rub the entire exterior with 1 tablespoon salt and the pepper. Line a 13" x 18" baking sheet with aluminum foil and place a wire rack on top. Place the goose on the wire rack and chill uncovered in the refrigerator for 10 hours.

2 Remove goose from refrigerator and allow to rest at room temperature for 30 minutes. Place oven racks in the top and bottom positions in the oven. Preheat oven to 350°F.

3 Rub the entire goose with olive oil, including inside the cavity (you do not need to separate the skin from the breast meat as you would for a turkey or chicken).

4 In a small bowl, stir together the remaining ½ tablespoon salt, onion powder, and minced sage leaves. Rub goose with seasoning mix. Fill the cavity of the bird with the quartered onion, sage sprigs, garlic, and ginger. Do not truss the legs (this will help the goose cook more evenly). Tuck the tips of the wings underneath the goose. Cook for 1 hour and 15 minutes.

5 Increase oven temperature to 450°F and cook for approximately 30 minutes more or until the internal temperature reaches 165°F.

6 Allow to rest for 30 minutes before serving.

Serve at a Victorian Christmas feast!

(Continued on next page)

Note: Goose can be pricey, but if you are willing to splurge, you'll reap the benefits for many meals to come. Pour the goose fat that collects in the bottom of the baking sheet through a strainer into a sealable jar and keep it in the fridge to use for roasting vegetables. After dinner, reserve the carcass and break it down into 3 to 4 pieces. Place it in a large pot with carrots, onions, garlic, fresh rosemary, and a couple of bay leaves. Fill the pot with cold water until the contents are covered. Heat on high until boiling, then reduce the heat to medium-low and simmer for 45 minutes. Strain the liquid into jars—now you have goose stock for making soup!

Be aware that the breast meat on a goose is smaller and darker than that of a chicken or turkey, so when you are carving the bird and see dark breast meat, don't worry that it's overcooked.

Chocolate Profiterole Christmas Puddings

Makes 26 mini profiteroles

"In half a minute Mrs. Cratchit entered—flushed, but smiling proudly—with the pudding, like a speckled cannon-ball, so hard and firm, blazing in half of half-a-quartern of ignited brandy, and bedight with Christmas holly stuck into the top."

Christmas puddings are a classic British holiday food, but steamed puddings can be fickle and time consuming. That's why I took the look and flavors of a traditional pudding and merged it with another dessert: the ever-popular cream puff.

INGREDIENTS

For the Brandy Pastry Cream
1 whole egg, plus 1 egg yolk
¼ cup sugar
1½ tablespoons cornstarch
2 pinches salt
1 cup whole milk
1 tablespoon brandy
1 teaspoon vanilla extract

For the Choux Pastry
½ cup flour
½ cup cocoa powder
¼ cup sugar
½ cup butter, softened
1 cup water
4 eggs, room temperature, thoroughly beaten

For the Icing
½ cup powdered sugar
1 tablespoon milk

For the Garnish
Cranberries
Mint leaves

INSTRUCTIONS

1 To make the brandy pastry cream, whisk together the egg, egg yolk, sugar, cornstarch, and salt in a bowl. Set aside. Bring the milk, brandy, and vanilla to a boil in a medium saucepan on medium heat, whisking regularly to prevent a skin and an overcooked bottom. Turn off heat. Very gradually whisk ¼ cup of the heated milk mix into the egg mix until fully incorporated. Whisk in another ¼ cup the same way. Gradually whisk the tempered egg mix into the rest of the milk mix.

2 Return to medium heat, whisking constantly for 2 minutes (the mixture will thicken slightly and start to bubble). Whisk for 1 minute more.

3 Remove from heat and transfer to a sealable container. Whisk while inside the container for 1 minute. Secure lid and chill for 90 minutes in the refrigerator, placing a layer of plastic wrap over the pastry cream after 20 minutes, making sure the plastic is in direct contact with the cream (this will prevent the cream from developing a skin).

4 To make the choux pastry, first move the oven racks to the top and bottom positions in the oven. Preheat oven to 400°F. Line 2 baking sheets with parchment paper and set aside. Sift together the flour, cocoa powder, and sugar in a bowl and set aside.

(Continued on page 19)

5 Melt the butter and water together in a medium saucepan on low heat. When the butter is fully melted, increase the heat to medium and bring to a boil. Turn off the heat and pour in the flour mix all at once. Stir together quickly with a silicone spatula. Turn heat back to medium. Cook for 2 minutes, stirring constantly. Remove from heat and transfer to a large mixing bowl. Beat in the eggs 1 tablespoon at a time with a hand mixer on medium speed. Beat until smooth.

6 Fit a piping bag with a ½-inch round piping tip and fill the bag with the pastry dough.

7 Pipe 13 (2-inch) mounds of dough at least 1½ inches apart on each baking sheet (2-inch mounds can be achieved by orienting the piping bag over the desired place on the baking sheet and applying even pressure to the bag for 10 seconds). Dip a finger in water and gently tap down the pointed peaks of the mounds.

8 Place the sheets in the oven. Bake for 20 minutes. Turn the heat down to 350°F and switch the positions of the pans, also rotating them. Bake for 20 minutes more. Turn off the heat and let the pastry shells sit for 10 minutes in the oven. Remove to a wire rack to cool.

9 Fit a piping bag with a ¼ inch round piping tip. Stir chilled pastry cream with a spoon and transfer to the piping bag. Cut a small "X" with a sharp knife in the bottom of each profiterole and insert piping tip through the "X." Fill each profiterole with cream.

10 To make the icing, whisk together the powdered sugar and milk in a small bowl until well combined. Spoon a small amount on top of each profiterole.

11 Top with cranberries and mint leaves to create the appearance of holly.

Serve at the Cratchit Christmas dinner!

Duchess Potatoes

"Master Peter Cratchit plunged a fork into the saucepan of potatoes, and getting the corners of his monstrous shirt collar . . . into his mouth, rejoiced to find himself so gallantly attired, and yearned to show his linen in the fashionable Parks."

These baked garlic mashed potato dollops hold a special surprise: a cheddar cheese center!

INGREDIENTS

- 1.5 lb. russet potatoes (approximately 4 medium potatoes)
- ½ cup butter (1 stick), divided
- 2 cloves garlic, minced
- 1 tablespoon milk
- ½ teaspoon salt
- ¼ teaspoon pepper
- 4 egg yolks
- 4 ounces mild cheddar cheese cubes

INSTRUCTIONS

1 Preheat oven to 425°F. Grease a baking sheet and set aside.

2 Peel the potatoes and cut them into quarters. Place in a medium saucepan and fill with cold water until the potatoes are under approximately 2 inches of water. Bring to a boil over medium heat and allow to boil for 15 minutes or until potatoes are fork-tender. Drain the water and transfer potatoes to a large mixing bowl.

3 Beat potatoes with an electric mixer on medium speed for 2 minutes. Add 6 tablespoons butter, garlic, milk, salt, and pepper. Beat until smooth. Beat in the egg yolks one at a time.

4 Transfer potato mix to a piping bag fitted with a large star tip. Pipe 21 (2-inch) solid circles, spaced evenly apart on the baking sheet.

5 Place a cheese square in the center of each circle and pipe a peak around and over the cheese, covering it.

6 Melt the remaining 2 tablespoons butter and sprinkle it over each peak with a pastry brush.

7 Bake for 20 minutes or until the edges begin to turn golden brown.

Serve at an elegant Christmas dinner!

Food for the Long Winter

The Chronicles of Narnia

By C. S. Lewis

*"It's she that makes it always winter. Always winter
and never Christmas; think of that!"*

Menu
Diggory's Apple Bites, 25
Turkey from Aslan's Table, 27
Turkish Delight, 29
Mrs. Beaver's Potatoes, 33

Diggory's Apple Bites

Makes 40 apple bites

"He knew which was the right tree at once, partly because it stood in the very centre and partly because the great silvery apples with which it was loaded shone so and cast a light of their own . . ."
—The Magician's Nephew

What better way to start a Narnian feast than with food from the creation of Narnia: apples! This easy appetizer offers a perfect balance of flavors: tart apple, creamy cheese, herbaceous thyme, and sweet honey.

INGREDIENTS

1 Honeycrisp apple
1 Granny Smith apple
1 pomegranate
4 ounces goat cheese
2 teaspoons milk
3–4 sprigs fresh thyme
Honey

INSTRUCTIONS

1 Core the apples and cut into 1/2-inch-thick slices and set aside. Cut the pomegranate in half and place in a large bowl of water. Peel inside the bowl (this helps prevent juice stains). Strain out seeds and set aside. Pinch the end of a sprig of thyme and slide fingers downward to remove leaves. Repeat with remaining sprigs. Discard stems and set leaves aside.

2 In a medium bowl, beat the goat cheese with a hand mixer on medium speed until crumbled. Add milk, beating until the mixture is smooth and spreadable.

3 Spread approximately 1/2 teaspoon goat cheese on each slice of apple. Sprinkle pomegranate seeds onto each apple. Sprinkle thyme leaves on the apple slices and top with a small drizzle of honey.

Serve to celebrate the creation of Narnia!

Turkey from Aslan's Table

Makes approximately 4 servings

"But on the table itself there was set out such a banquet as had never been seen. . . . There were turkeys and geese and peacocks, there were boars' heads and sides of venison . . . and the smell of the fruit and the wine blew toward them like a promise of all happiness."
—The Voyage of the *Dawn Treader*

Bone-in turkey breast is a great alternative to a whole turkey if you're not feeding a large crowd. This honey- and lemon-glazed dish pairs beautifully with blackberry wine sauce.

INGREDIENTS

For the Turkey
1 (4-lb.) frozen bone-in
   turkey breast, thawed
1 tablespoon olive oil
1 tablespoon lemon zest
2 teaspoons kosher salt
½ teaspoon pepper
½ cup honey
1 tablespoon fresh
   lemon juice

For the Blackberry Sauce
1 lb. frozen blackberries
1 cup sweet
   blackberry wine
1 tablespoon lemon zest
1 tablespoon lemon juice
2 teaspoons sugar
½ teaspoon
   ground ginger
¼ teaspoon kosher salt

Special Tools
Wire-mesh strainer

INSTRUCTIONS

1 To make the turkey, line a baking sheet with aluminum foil and set aside. Move oven racks to the top and bottom positions in the oven. Preheat oven to 350°F. Rinse turkey and pat dry. Place the turkey on the baking sheet and rub with olive oil, gently separating the skin from the breast meat with your fingers. In a small bowl, stir together the lemon zest, salt, and pepper. Rub turkey with seasoning mix, including under the skin and inside the cavity.

2 In a small bowl, whisk together honey and lemon juice until well combined. Brush turkey with honey mix, including under the skin. Tuck in any overhanging skin around the wing areas. Overhanging skin above the neck can be tucked under the skin below the neck hole (you may need to gently separate it from the meat with your fingers to create a pocket).

3 Roast for 1 hour.* After 30 minutes, rotate pan and begin glazing turkey every 15 minutes. When the hour is up, increase heat to 450°F and roast 20 to 30 minutes more or until internal temperature reaches 170°F on a meat thermometer (continuing to glaze every 15 minutes). If necessary, tent the top of the breasts with aluminum foil during the last 20 minutes to prevent overbrowning. Allow to rest for 30 minutes.

4 To make the blackberry sauce, combine all ingredients in a medium saucepan over medium-high heat. Bring to a boil, stirring occasionally. Reduce heat to medium-low

(Continued on next page)

and simmer 15 minutes, stirring occasionally. Mash the blackberries with a potato masher or the bottom of a heavy glass cup. Strain the mixture, pressing the fruit through the strainer with a spoon. Scrape the bottom of the strainer to be sure to get all the fruit pulp as well. Return the strained mixture to the pan and discard contents of strainer. Simmer 10 minutes more. Remove from heat and allow to rest for 15 minutes.

Serve to the weary travelers of the Dawn Treader!

*If your turkey breast is top-heavy and won't stand upright on its own, you can prop it up by placing two small oven-safe bowls (such as ramekins) against the sides.

Turkish Delight

Makes 32 pieces

"The Queen let another drop fall from her bottle on to the snow, and instantly there appeared a round box . . . which, when opened, turned out to contain several pounds of the best Turkish Delight. Each piece was sweet and light to the very centre and Edmund had never tasted anything more delicious."
—The Lion, the Witch, and the Wardrobe

Turkish delight is a dish that fascinates many, but its traditional flavor combinations (like rose and pistachio) can be daunting to people trying it for the first time. This recipe has a simple lemon flavor, making it more accessible to those who are new to it. Many Turkish delight recipes are also quite complicated, requiring hours of simmering and special tools like candy thermometers. This recipe, however, is Turkish delight made easy! The key lies in allowing the gelatin to simmer with the sugar mix, instead of adding it later. The result is a simple, forgiving recipe with few ingredients. The final product is sweet, chewy, and very soft—a delicious introduction to the food of Narnia!

INGREDIENTS

2 cups sugar
¾ cup cold water
2 packets gelatin (a little under 1½ tablespoons)
1½ teaspoons fresh lemon juice
2 teaspoons lemon extract
2 drops yellow food coloring
½ cup powdered sugar
½ cup cornstarch

INSTRUCTIONS

1 Very generously coat a 10" x 5" metal loaf pan with cooking spray and flour. Set aside. Gently stir the sugar, cold water, and gelatin in a medium saucepan until combined. Heat the mixture on medium heat until the sugar dissolves, stirring regularly. Bring the mixture to a boil, and then immediately turn the heat down to low (keep a close eye on it—the mixture will start to foam upward quickly when it starts to boil and could overflow if allowed to continue). Simmer for 10 minutes without stirring.

2 Remove from heat. Quickly stir in the lemon juice, extract, and food coloring. *Be careful, as the sugar mix is very hot and will foam upward slightly.*

3 Quickly pour the mix into the prepared pan and chill in the refrigerator for 4 to 6 hours.

4 Whisk the powdered sugar and cornstarch in a medium bowl. Sprinkle a generous layer of the sugar-cornstarch mix onto a cutting board. Loosen the candy mix from the edges of the pan with a sharp knife coated with cooking spray. Overturn the candy onto the cutting board (you may need to ease it up from the bottom of the pan with

(Continued on page 31)

the knife before overturning). Cut the mixture into squares approximately 1 inch across, respraying the knife if it starts to stick. Very gently toss the pieces in the powdered sugar mix to coat.

5 These can be eaten right away. The pieces can also be allowed to set overnight on a shallow bed of the sugar-cornstarch mix in a large, lightly covered dish with tall sides (like a glass baking dish). Overnight setting will achieve a slightly more stable consistency.

Serve to any Sons of Adam or Daughters of Eve you find wandering through Narnia's winter woodland!

Mrs. Beaver's Potatoes

Makes 15 potatoes

*"The potatoes are on boiling and the kettle's singing and I daresay,
Mr. Beaver, you'll get us some fish."*
—Mrs. Beaver, The Lion, the Witch, and the Wardrobe

These salty, savory mashed-then-roasted potatoes are sure to disappear even more quickly at your Christmas gathering than they did when Mrs. Beaver fed them to the hungry Pevensies.

INGREDIENTS

15 baby Yukon Gold potatoes
½ teaspoon kosher salt, divided
¼ cup butter
½ tablespoon lemon juice
¼ teaspoon fresh ground black pepper
1–2 teaspoons snipped fresh chives

INSTRUCTIONS

1 Preheat oven to 425°F. Grease two baking sheets and set aside.

2 Add potatoes to a large pot and fill with cold water until approximately 1 inch above the top of the potatoes. Add ¼ teaspoon kosher salt and bring to a boil over medium-high heat. Boil for 10 to 15 minutes until potatoes are fork-tender. Drain and transfer potatoes to the baking sheets, placing the potatoes evenly apart.

3 Smash potatoes with a potato masher or the bottom of a heavy glass. Melt the butter and stir in lemon juice until combined. Generously brush potatoes with melted butter mix. Sprinkle on pepper and remaining salt.

4 Bake 15 to 20 minutes or until edges are golden brown and beginning to crisp. Sprinkle with chives.

Serve to the future kings and queens of Narnia!

Christmas with the March Family

Little Women

By Louisa May Alcott

"The December snow fell quietly without, and the fire crackled cheerfully within. It was a comfortable room . . . books filled the recesses, chrysanthemums and Christmas roses bloomed in the windows, and a pleasant atmosphere of home peace pervaded it."

Menu

Rustic Whole Wheat Bread, 37

Turkey Roulade, 39

Baked Apples, 43

Jo's Gingerbread, 44

Rustic Whole Wheat Bread

Makes 1 (8-inch) round loaf

"When they went away, leaving comfort behind, I think there were not in all the city four merrier people than the hungry little girls who gave away their breakfasts and contented themselves with bread and milk on Christmas morning."

A rustic wheat loaf is just the right bread for a wholesome family Christmas like the one shared by the March family in *Little Women*. This one is sweetened with molasses for extra holiday cheer.

INGREDIENTS

¼ cup molasses
1½ cups warm water
1 (7-g) packet active
   dry yeast
3¼ cups whole wheat
   flour, plus extra
   for kneading
2 teaspoons salt
1 egg
1 tablespoon butter

INSTRUCTIONS

1 Add molasses to the warm water and stir until completely dissolved. Add yeast to warm water and allow to rest 5 minutes, stirring gently after 1 to 2 minutes.

2 Add flour to the bowl of a standing mixer fitted with a dough hook and pour the salt to one side of the flour. Add the egg and the water mix to the other side of the flour and beat on medium-low until combined, raising the mixer speed momentarily to incorporate the last bit of flour on the bottom if necessary.

3 Scrape dough onto a floured surface. Lightly dust dough and hands with flour and knead for approximately 6 minutes, reflouring work surface and hands frequently.

4 Shape the dough into a boule by first flattening the dough into a circle that stands about half as high as before. Flip the dough over so that whatever side was on the bottom while kneading is now on top. Fold the top of the circle down into the center, pressing to adhere. Rotate

(Continued on next page.)

circle 90° and repeat, taking care to press together where the folds overlap to avoid air pockets. Rotate and repeat 2 more times. Flip the dough back over so that the "seam" is on the bottom. Cupping your hands, slide them about 2 inches under the bottom of the dough to create more surface tension and round out the shape. Rotate the dough and slide cupped hands underneath again, repeating until the entire circumference has been tightened and shaped. Allow to rest for 10 minutes. Gently degas the dough and reshape into a boule (you can degas by pressing down all over the dough until it stands about half as high as before and creates a 7-inch-wide circle, then flipping it over so the seam will be on the same side as before).

5 Grease a large bowl. Place dough in the bowl, turning once to coat so that it is sitting in the bowl seam-side up. Cover with a clean kitchen cloth and allow to rise 1 hour in a warm place. Preheat oven to 375°F.*

6 On a lightly floured surface, turn dough out of the bowl and punch down. Flip dough back over (seam-side up) and re-shape into a boule. Place on a baking sheet lined with parchment paper. Cover with a clean cloth and allow to rest for 45 minutes.

7 Slice a decorative slit across the top of the dough with a sharp knife, cutting about ¹/₂ inch into the dough.**

8 Melt butter and brush it over the top and sides of the dough. Bake for 40 minutes or until brown and the loaf sounds hollow when firmly tapped on the bottom. Remove to a wire rack to cool.

Serve on a cheery Christmas morning!

*When making bread, the kitchen shouldn't be any colder than 71°F. If your kitchen is cold in the winter, letting the dough rise near (but not on) the preheated oven can help keep it warm.

**For best results, keep the decoration simple. The loaf pictured has 1 curved line across one side of the top of the loaf with small lines about 2 inches apart radiating out from it on either side.

Turkey Roulade

Makes 2 roulades

"There never was such a Christmas dinner as they had that day. The fat turkey was a sight to behold, when Hannah sent him up, stuffed, browned, and decorated . . ."

Turkey roulade is an elegant alternative to the traditional roasted holiday turkey. Feel free to experiment with your favorite dried fruits and nuts for the filling to make it your own!

INGREDIENTS

For the Glaze
¾ cup cranberry juice
2 tablespoons brown sugar, packed
1 teaspoon lemon juice
¼ teaspoon thyme
¼ teaspoon rosemary
¼ teaspoon salt
Pinch black pepper

For the Roulades
2 boneless frozen (1-lb.) turkey breasts, thawed
1 heaping cup Bartlett pears, cubed
1 cup high-quality white bread, cubed
¼ cup dried cranberries
¼ cup chopped walnuts, toasted
¼ cup yellow onion, finely chopped
½ teaspoon rosemary
¼ teaspoon thyme
¼ teaspoon salt
⅛ teaspoon pepper
¼ cup chicken broth
2 tablespoons melted butter

Special Tools
Meat mallet
Kitchen twine

INSTRUCTIONS

1 Preheat oven to 375°F. Line a baking sheet with aluminum foil and place a wire rack on top. Set aside.

2 To prepare the glaze, combine all the glaze ingredients in a small saucepan over medium heat and bring to a boil. Turn heat down to medium-low and simmer for 15 minutes. Remove from heat and set aside.

3 To prepare the roulades, carefully separate the skin from the turkey meat (try to avoid making any holes or tears) and set it aside. If meat is not uniformly thick, cut it width-wise through the thick portion, stopping about 1 inch from the end, and unfold.

4 Place the first breast between two sheets of plastic wrap, with the skinned side of the breast on the bottom, and pound with a meat mallet until it is half its original thickness. Repeat the process with the second turkey breast. Set aside.

5 Add all the remaining roulade ingredients except the broth and butter to a large bowl to make the stuffing. Stir until thoroughly combined. Pour in your chicken broth and butter, stirring until well-coated.

6 Remove the plastic wrap from the first turkey breast. Lay it flat on a cutting board (skinned-side down) and spread a layer of stuffing evenly across the top, leaving about ½ inch around the edge uncovered. Starting at a narrow end, roll the turkey breast into a spiral. Cut the turkey skin in half and wrap one half as tightly as possible over the top of the roulade without tearing it. Don't worry if the skin doesn't reach all the way around to the bottom of the roulade.

(Continued on page 41)

7 Cut 4 lengths of kitchen twine, each about 14 inches long. Working one length at a time, hold both ends of the twine and slide the middle under the roulade. Pull the first length of twine along the roulade until it is about 1 inch from the far end, then tie it tightly in place with a double knot. Repeat the process for the remaining three lengths of twine, keeping them 1 to 2 inches apart across the entire roulade. Brush the roulade with glaze.

8 Repeat Steps 6 and 7 for the second turkey breast.

9 Set the roulades on the wire rack and place the rack in the oven. Cook for 45 to 60 minutes or until a food thermometer inserted in the center of each roulade reads 160°F, brushing them every 10 to 15 minutes with the remaining glaze. If the skin begins to overbrown, tuck a piece of aluminum foil over the roulade for the rest of the cooking time.

10 Let the roulades rest for 10 to 15 minutes while lightly covered in tinfoil before cutting.

Serve to the March Family on Christmas Morning!

Baked Apples

Makes 8 apples

"This was Jo's favorite refuge, and here she loved to retire with half a dozen russets and a nice book, to enjoy the quiet and the society of a pet rat who lived near by and didn't mind her a particle."

Elevate a simple fruit to the level of a delicious dessert with this easy baked apple recipe. It's a perfect opportunity to get children involved in the kitchen. They'll love filling the hollowed apples and drizzling on the molasses!

INGREDIENTS

8 Gala apples
½ cup rolled oats
½ cup brown sugar, packed
½ cup cranberries
½ cup sliced almonds, coarsely crushed
2 teaspoons cinnamon
½ teaspoon allspice
1 cup full-flavor molasses
Extra molasses, if needed

INSTRUCTIONS

1 Preheat oven to 375°F. Line a 9" x 13" high-walled baking pan with foil and set aside.

2 Slice the top off each apple and use a melon baller to scoop out the core, leaving the bottom and most of the flesh intact. In a medium bowl, stir together all remaining ingredients except molasses until well combined and brown sugar is broken up into small pieces.

3 Place the apples in the baking pan. Add 2 spoonfuls of filling to each apple. Pour 1 tablespoon molasses over the filling. Add enough filling to fill each apple. Pour 1 tablespoon of molasses over the top of each apple.

4 Bake 45 to 50 minutes or until apples are soft, drizzling extra molasses over the top if the filling starts to look dried out.

Serve to your favorite literary heroine!

Jo's Gingerbread

Makes 30 cookies

"The things were just what I wanted, and all the better for being made instead of bought. Beth's new 'ink bib' was capital, and Hannah's box of hard gingerbread will be a treasure."
—Jo

The instructions here explain how to decorate your cookies to look like the four March sisters, but you can also decorate your gingerbread however you like. If you're feeling ambitious, you can even make other characters from the book: Laurie, Marmie, John Brooke, Professor Bhaer, and even Meg's children!

INGREDIENTS

4 cups flour
1½ teaspoons
    baking soda
2¼ teaspoons ginger
1¼ teaspoons cinnamon
½ teaspoon allspice
¾ teaspoon
    ground cloves
½ teaspoon salt
½ cup unsalted butter,
    softened
¼ cup shortening
½ cup brown sugar,
    packed
¼ cup granulated sugar
1 egg
¾ cup molasses
Icing and sprinkles in
    various colors

Special Tools
3" x 3½" gingerbread
    woman cookie cutter
Food Pen

INSTRUCTIONS

1 In a medium bowl, stir together the first 7 ingredients and set aside.

2 Cream the butter, shortening, and sugars in a standing mixer on medium speed until smooth. Beat in the egg and molasses. Gradually beat in the dry mix until combined, stopping to scrape the bowl if necessary.

3 Gather the dough into a ball and cover with plastic wrap. Chill in the refrigerator for 2½ hours or until easy to handle. While you wait, preheat oven to 350°F.

4 Between two sheets of wax paper, roll out half the dough to a little under ¼-inch thickness (wrap the remaining dough in plastic wrap and chill in the refrigerator until ready to use). Keeping the paper in place, lay the rolled dough on a baking sheet and chill in the refrigerator for 10 minutes. Remove the top sheet of wax paper and discard. Use a cookie cutter to cut out gingerbread women shapes. If you would like the Meg cookies to have their hair in a bun like the ones shown in the picture, shape small scraps of dough into circles and gently press them on top of the heads of one quarter of the gingerbread women.

5 Place cookies 2 inches apart on a baking sheet lined with parchment paper (if the shapes are too delicate to lift from the paper without tearing, slide an offset spatula or frosting knife underneath to lift them). Bake for 7 minutes or until the edges are set. Allow the cookies to cool for 5 minutes on the baking sheet before moving them to a wire rack to cool completely.

6 Roll, cut out, and bake remaining cookies from second half of dough. Repeat the process with the scraps of dough.

7 Decorate with icing and sprinkles to look like the four March sisters:

- **FOR MEG** Outline and fill the dress using purple icing. Add white pearl sprinkles while the icing is still wet. Draw the face with a food pen and outline the head and the top of the hair bun with chocolate icing.
- **FOR JO** Outline and fill in the dress using white icing, then trace a crisscross pattern on top with blue icing. Draw the face with a food pen. Make the curls around her head by drawing a loop pattern with chocolate icing. For the braid, draw a zigzag line one way over her shoulder and draw another zigzag over it going the opposite way. Finish the braid with a blue icing bow.
- **FOR BETH** Outline and fill the dress using teal icing, then use white icing and some white pearl sprinkles to make a Peter Pan collar with buttons. Draw the face with a food pen. Pipe her hair with chocolate icing by starting below her shoulder, going over her head, and ending below her opposite shoulder. Add a dot of teal icing for a pin in her hair.
- **FOR AMY** Outline and fill the dress using pink icing. Scatter multicolored sprinkles over it before it dries. Draw the face with a food pen. Pipe her hair with yellow icing by starting below her shoulder and piping a zigzag line over her head and ending below her opposite shoulder. Pipe another line over it, zigzagging in the opposite direction to give her hair a wavy look. Draw a blue icing bow in her hair.

Serve to a young writer who is just starting out on her own!

Feast of the Sugar Plum Fairy

"The Nutcracker and the Mouse King"

By E. T. A. Hoffmann

"At that moment a silvery-bright bell rang ding-a-ling, the doors flew open, and such a flood of light streamed in from the big parlor. . . . Papa and Mama appeared in the doorway, took their children by the hand, and said, 'Come in, come in, dear children, and see what the Christ Child has brought you.'"

Menu

Garlic Rosemary Toasted Almonds, 49

Pesto and Bacon Puff Pastry Christmas Tree, 51

Mouse King Cheese Bites, 55

Sugar Plums, 57

Garlic Rosemary Toasted Almonds

Makes 1 cup almonds

"At her father's bidding, Marie put in a nut, and—crack—the little man bit it in two, the shell fell down, and Marie found the sweet kernel in her hand."

These easy almonds can be served warm as an appetizer or packaged and given as a gift.

INGREDIENTS

1 cup almonds
1 tablespoon olive oil
1 tablespoon honey
1 clove garlic, minced
1 teaspoon fresh
   rosemary, minced
1 teaspoon kosher salt
$1/8$ teaspoon pepper

INSTRUCTIONS

1 Preheat oven to 325°F. Line a baking sheet with parchment paper and set aside.

2 Combine all ingredients in a large bowl and stir until the almonds are well coated. Transfer contents of bowl to the baking sheet, spreading it out in a single layer.

3 Toast for 15 minutes, stirring halfway through. Allow nuts to cool on the pan for 10 minutes.

Serve warm at the start of a magical meal!

Pesto and Bacon Puff Pastry Christmas Tree

Makes 1 (10-inch) tree

"The big Christmas tree in the middle of the room was decorated with any number of gold and silver apples, and sugared almonds, bright-colored candles, and goodies of all kinds . . . and the tree itself, shining with an inner light, invited the children to pick its blossoms and fruits."

This impressive pastry is deceptively easy to make and bakes in only 20 minutes. The perfect way to feed a hungry crowd at Christmas!

INGREDIENTS

- 8 slices center-cut bacon
- 2 sheets frozen puff pastry, thawed
- ¼ cup pesto (make your own using ½ batch of the recipe on page 244)
- ½ cup shredded mozzarella cheese
- 1 egg mixed with 1 tablespoon water, for egg wash

INSTRUCTIONS

1 Preheat the oven to 375°F. Cut bacon into bits and fry until cooked but not crispy. Transfer to a plate lined with a paper towel and set aside.

2 Roll puff pastry sheets into 10-inch squares. Place 1 sheet on a greased baking sheet. Spread a layer of pesto across the pastry sheet in the shape of a giant triangle, keeping the pesto at least 2 inches from the bottom of the pastry and at least 1 inch from all remaining sides. Spread a small rectangle of pesto at the bottom of the triangle (this will be the trunk), keeping it at least 1 inch from the bottom of the pastry.

(Continued on next page)

3 Sprinkle bacon bits and cheese over the pesto. Brush exposed pastry with egg wash. Place the remaining puff pastry sheet on top, pressing gently to adhere. Cut away the un-filled portion of pastry, leaving about 1 inch between the filling and the trimmed edge of the pastry. You should be left with a large tree shape.

4 Starting at the bottom of the triangle and working up, use a sharp knife to cut 1-inch-wide strips along one side of the triangle, stopping about 1 inch from the center of the tree. Do the same with the other side (this will create the branches and a 2-inch "trunk").

5 Brush the tree with egg wash. Twist each "branch" into a spiral.

6 Place the baking sheet in your oven and bake for about 20 minutes or until the top of the pastry begins to turn golden brown. Allow to cool for 5 to 10 minutes on the pan.

Serve warm on a magical Christmas night!

Tip: No need to throw away puff pastry scraps! Simply cut into 1-inch-wide strips, brush with melted butter, and sprinkle with cinnamon and sugar. Twist each strip multiple times and place in a 375° oven on a greased baking sheet until puffed and light golden brown.

Mouse King Cheese Bites

Makes 8 cheese bites

"The King of Mice charged him. Marie was beside herself. . . . Without quite knowing what she was doing, she took off her left shoe and flung it with all her might into the thick of the enemy, hoping to hit their king. In that moment, everything vanished from Marie's sight."

Sometimes the best recipes don't involve any cooking at all. These cheese bites are quick to assemble and will disappear off the plate just as quickly!

INGREDIENTS

- 8 white cheddar spreadable cheese wedges
- 8 square wheat crackers
- 16 almond slices
- 16 whole black peppercorns
- 1 grape tomato
- 1 cucumber
- 1 large sprig fresh rosemary (48 leaves needed)
- 1 slice cheddar cheese

INSTRUCTIONS

1 Place the cheese wedges flat on the crackers.

2 For ears, insert 2 almond slices on top of each cheese wedge at the base of the triangle. For eyes, place 2 peppercorns in the middle of each triangle.

3 For the nose, cut 8 tiny triangles from the tomato and place them on the triangle tip of each cheese wedge. For the tails, cut 8 (4-inch) slivers from the cucumber and insert them into the back of each cheese wedge, making a hole with a toothpick if necessary.

4 For whiskers, insert two rosemary leaves on either side of the triangle tip, under the tomato nose.

5 For the crowns, cut 8 (1/4" x 1/2") rectangles from the slice of cheddar. Cut 2 small triangles from the top length of each rectangle. Prop a crown against each set of almond ears.

Enjoy while watching the latest production of The Nutcracker!

Sugar Plums

Makes 16 sugar plums

"Then they brought in the most wonderful fruit and candy Marie had ever seen and began with their snow-white hands to squeeze the fruit, crush the spices, and grate the sugared almonds."

Don't let their humble appearance fool you; these Byzantine-style sugar plums are packed with a rich, spiced, and lightly sweet flavor. Plus, they are faster and easier to make than the traditional Victorian variety—ready to eat in just two steps! They use traditional Byzantine fruits and nuts, but I added a splash of rum to shake things up a little.

INGREDIENTS

½ cup pistachios
½ cup pitted dates
¼ cup prunes
¼ cup dried cherries
¼ cup dried figs,
   stems removed
1 teaspoon orange zest
½ teaspoon cinnamon
1 pinch kosher salt
2 teaspoons spiced rum
¼ cup turbinado sugar

Special Tools
Food processor

INSTRUCTIONS

1 Add all ingredients except the rum and sugar to a food processor on low for 1 to 2 minutes until everything is broken into very small pieces. Add in the rum and pulse for 15 seconds until well combined.

2 Shape fruit mix into balls approximately 1¼ inches wide. Roll in sugar until well-coated. Store in an airtight container at room temperature until ready to serve.

Serve to the Sugar Plum Fairy after she completes her famous dance!

Hearty Wilderness Fare

White Fang

By Jack London

"To have a full stomach, to daze lazily in the sunshine—such things were remuneration in full for his ardors and toils. . . . They were expressions of life, and life is always happy when it is expressing itself."

Menu

Arctic Trail Coffee Muffins, 61

Seared Salmon with Lemon Dill Butter, 63

White Whiskey Baked Beans with Bacon, 65

S'mores Baked Alaska, 67

Arctic Trail Coffee Muffins

Makes 12 muffins

"Henry did not reply, but munched on in silence, until, the meal finished, he topped it with a final cup of coffee. He wiped his mouth with the back of his hand. . . . A long wailing cry, fiercely sad, from somewhere in the darkness, had interrupted him."

These muffins taste delicious with maple butter. To make your own maple butter, simply mix a few tablespoons of maple syrup into a stick of softened butter until smooth.

INGREDIENTS

½ cup unsalted butter
2 teaspoons instant
  coffee granules
1 cup milk
2 cups flour
½ cup granulated sugar
¼ cup brown sugar,
  packed
2 teaspoons
  baking powder
¼ teaspoon each
  cinnamon, ginger,
  and nutmeg
½ teaspoon salt
2 tablespoons
  maple syrup
1 egg
1 teaspoon vanilla extract

INSTRUCTIONS

1 Preheat oven to 375°F. Melt the butter in a microwave and set aside to cool. Stir the instant coffee granules into the milk and allow to dissolve. Fill a muffin pan with liners and set aside.

2 In a large bowl, whisk together the flour, sugars, baking powder, spices, and salt. Whisk in the maple syrup, egg, vanilla, melted butter, and milk mix (stir the milk thoroughly before pouring it in).

3 Fill the muffin liners until ³/₄ full. Bake for 20 minutes or until a toothpick inserted in the center comes out clean. Remove the muffins from the pan and allow to cool for 20 minutes on a wire rack.

Serve warm on a cold Alaskan morning!

Seared Salmon with Lemon Dill Butter

Makes 4 salmon fillets

"Contented sounds saluted his ear. . . . And there was a smell in the air of fish. There was food. The famine was gone. He came out boldly from the forest and trotted into camp straight to Grey Beaver's tepee. . . . Kloo-kooch welcomed him with glad cries and the whole of a fresh-caught fish."

Enliven a simple salmon fillet by topping it with aromatic, zesty lemon dill butter.

INGREDIENTS

4 (8-oz.) salmon fillets, skin on
2 tablespoons vegetable oil
1 teaspoon salt, divided
Freshly ground black pepper
¼ cup lemon dill butter (See recipe on page 237)

INSTRUCTIONS

1 To prepare the salmon, remove any pin bones from the fillets if necessary. Pat down the fillets with a paper towel to dry.

2 Heat oil in a cast-iron skillet on medium-high heat until it sizzles strongly when flecked with a few drops of water. Reduce heat to medium-low.

3 Place 1 fillet skin-side-down in the hot oil and hold down with a spatula for 1 minute. Sprinkle on ⅛ teaspoon salt and 4 twists of pepper. Allow to cook for up to 6 minutes more, depending on the thickness of the fillet. You should be able to lift the fillet from the pan with the spatula without sticking. If it still sticks, allow it to cook for another minute.

4 Flip the fillet and sprinkle with the same amount of salt and pepper as before. Allow to cook for 3 minutes or until the meat is very pale peach throughout and the internal temperature reaches 120°F. Transfer to a serving plate.

5 Repeat Steps 2 to 4 with the remaining plain butter, fillets, and seasoning. Add approximately 1 tablespoon lemon dill butter to the top of each of your fillets.

Serve after a long trek through the wilderness!

White Whiskey Baked Beans with Bacon

Makes 11 cups

"Henry was bending over and adding ice to the babbling pot of beans when he was startled. . . . He straightened up in time to see a dim form disappearing across the snow into the shelter of the dark."

This recipe swaps the heavier, more tomato-ey flavors of traditional baked beans for lighter additions like garlic, onion, and maple.

INGREDIENTS

1 lb. great northern beans

1 lb. navy beans

1 lb. bacon

2 tablespoons melted bacon fat (reserved from bacon)

1 sweet onion

3 cloves garlic, minced

¾ teaspoon salt

¼ teaspoon pepper

10 cups chicken stock

2 tablespoons whiskey

3 tablespoons maple syrup

1 tablespoon snipped fresh parsley

INSTRUCTIONS

1 Rinse each set of beans and soak separately in 6 cups of water for 8 hours.

2 Drain the water and transfer beans to a large pot. Cut the bacon into bits and fry. Transfer to a plate lined with a paper towel. Cover and chill in the refrigerator until ready to use. Reserve 2 tablespoons of the bacon fat.

3 Dice the onion and add to the pot, along with the bacon fat, garlic, salt, pepper, and chicken stock. Stir to combine.

4 Bring to a boil over high heat. Reduce heat to medium-low and simmer for 4 hours, stirring every 10 minutes, until beans are soft and most of the liquid has evaporated. Remove from heat. Stir in whiskey, maple syrup, parsley, and bacon bits.

Serve to your fellow explorers as you take a break from blazing new trails in the Alaskan wilderness!

Note: In this recipe, the beans need to soak for 8 hours before cooking and simmer for 4 hours.

S'mores Baked Alaska

Makes 1 baked Alaska

*"He could not immediately forego his wild heritage and his memories of the Wild.
There were days when he crept to the edge of the forest and stood and listened to
something calling him far and away."*

This easy take on traditional baked Alaska skips a step by replacing the cake layer with graham cracker.

INGREDIENTS

12 graham crackers
4 cups chocolate ice cream, softened to spreading consistency
2 cups marshmallow fluff
8 pasteurized egg whites, room temperature
2 teaspoons vanilla extract
1½ teaspoons cream of tartar
¼ teaspoon salt
2¼ cups powdered sugar
¼ cup mini marshmallows
¼ cup graham cracker pieces
¼ cup milk chocolate chunks

Special Tools

Chef's torch (optional)

INSTRUCTIONS

1 Line a 5" x 9" loaf pan with plastic wrap, making sure the wrap extends well over the sides.

2 Make a single layer of 4 graham crackers in the bottom of the pan, trimming to fit if necessary. Add 2 scoops of chocolate ice cream and spread into an even layer. Add 1 cup marshmallow fluff and spread into an even layer. Add another layer of graham crackers.

3 Repeat Step 2, starting with the ice cream.

4 Fold the ends of the plastic wrap over the final layer of graham crackers and place in a freezer for at least 3 hours.

5 In the bowl of a standing mixer fitted with a whisk attachment, beat the egg whites, vanilla, cream of tartar, and salt on medium speed for 3 minutes or until soft peaks form.

6 With the mixer running, very gradually add the powdered sugar. Set mixer to full speed and continue to beat for 5 minutes or until stiff peaks form. The meringue should be bright white and glossy and should feel smooth when rubbed between two fingers. Transfer approximately 1 cup of meringue to a small bowl and set aside. Transfer the remainder of the meringue to a large piping bag fitted with a large star tip (such as a Wilton #1M tip).

7 Fold back the wrap from the graham layer and overturn the frozen loaf pan onto a heat-safe serving tray. Remove the pan and plastic wrap.

8 Working quickly, spread the 1 cup of reserved meringue on top of the ice cream loaf in a flat layer. Using the piping

(Continued on next page)

bag, pipe tight squiggles of meringue along the sides of the loaf, making sure not to leave any of the loaf exposed. Pipe a line around the upper edge of the loaf to cover where the flat top and squiggles meet.

9 Lightly toast the meringue with a chef's torch. Alternatively, place the baked Alaska in an oven under a 550°F broiler for 2 minutes. The broiler method achieves a lighter, more even toasted color, while the torch is darker and accentuates the lines of the meringue. If using the broiler method, be sure the baked Alaska is on an oven-safe serving tray and chill the tray in the refrigerator for 20 minutes before plating.

10 Sprinkle top of baked Alaska with mini marshmallows, graham cracker pieces, and milk chocolate chunks.

Serve while listening for the faint call of the wild in the distance!

Note: Meringue can be finicky. Even a little bit of moisture or fat can ruin it. To ensure success, make sure all tools are clean and dry, use liquid egg whites instead of whole eggs to avoid broken yolks, and cook in a kitchen no warmer than 70°F with low humidity.

Thanksgiving

While the focus of Christmas seems to always be on presents, the cornerstone of Thanksgiving is the notion of hospitality. This idea of offering aid to family, friends, and even strangers, and welcoming them into the home plays a vital role in many classic literary works. In the Little House series by Laura Ingalls Wilder, holidays like Thanksgiving are a vital time for pioneers and homesteaders to build new community ties to replace the neighbors and family they have left behind. Even books set in mythical lands that do not explicitly feature Thanksgiving portray key scenes where characters open up their homes and their larders in an act of hospitality. Think of Beorn in *The Hobbit* and the beasts of Redwall Abbey in the *Redwall* books.

So, bake up a loaf of Beorn's Honey Nut Banana Bread or Redwall Abbey's Deeper 'N Ever Pie and throw open the front door! After all, the gift of feeling welcome knows no season.

A Long-Expected Thanksgiving

The Hobbit

By J. R. R. Tolkien

"There were many people there, elvish-looking folk. . . .
There was a fire in their midst and there were torches fastened
to some of the trees round about; but most splendid sight of all:
they were eating and drinking and laughing merrily."

Menu

Beorn's Honey Nut Banana Bread, 75

Melton Mowbray: Mini Pork Pies, 77

Hobbit Door Giant Chocolate Chip Cookie, 79

Bag End Orchard Salad, 83

Beorn's Honey Nut Banana Bread

Makes 1 loaf

"[Beorn] lives in an oak-wood and has a great wooden house; and as a man he keeps cattle and horses which are nearly as marvelous as himself. They work for him and talk to him. . . . He keeps hives and hives of great fierce bees; and lives most on cream and honey."
—Gandalf

Beorn may be a tough nut to crack, but he can make a mean meal! Below is my own interpretation of the bread and honey he serves Thorin's company when they stay at his home on the edge of Mirkwood Forest.

INGREDIENTS

1¼ cups flour
½ teaspoon baking soda
⅛ teaspoon salt
¼ teaspoon cinnamon
¼ teaspoon ginger
2 brown bananas
¼ cup granulated sugar
¼ cup brown sugar, packed
3 tablespoons honey
½ teaspoon vanilla extract
1 egg, lightly beaten
¼ cup melted butter, cooled
¼ cup walnut chips

INSTRUCTIONS

1 Preheat oven to 350°F. Coat a loaf pan with cooking spray and set aside.

2 In a large bowl, whisk together flour, baking soda, salt, cinnamon, and ginger. Create a well in the center of the flour mix. Set aside.

3 In a medium bowl, mash the bananas with a fork. Stir in the sugars, honey, vanilla, egg, and melted butter.

4 Add the wet mix to the well in the center of the dry mix. Stir until just combined. Stir in the walnuts.

5 Pour the mix into the loaf pan and bake for 45 minutes or until a toothpick inserted in the center comes out clean.

6 Allow to cool in the pan for 10 minutes. Loosen the loaf from the pan along the edges with a butter knife and overturn the loaf onto a wire rack. Allow to rest upright until completely cool (approximately 1 hour).

7 Wrap the loaf in plastic wrap and store at room temperature for 1 day before serving.

Serve to a disgruntled shapeshifter to thank him for protecting you from goblins!

Melton Mowbray: Mini Pork Pies

Makes 8 mini pork pies

"'I hope there is something left for the late-comers to eat and drink! What's that? Tea! No thank you! A little red wine, I think, for me.' 'And for me,' said Thorin. 'And raspberry jam and apple-tart,' said Bifur. 'And mince-pies and cheese,' said Bofur. 'And pork-pie and salad,' said Bombur."

Don't worry too much about achieving the perfect crimped edge on these pies. The rustic look is part of the charm!

INGREDIENTS

For the Filling
1½ lb. pork loin, cut into
   ½–¾-inch cubes
1 onion, minced
3 cloves garlic, minced
2 teaspoons fresh
   rosemary leaves,
   chopped
1 teaspoon salt
¼ teaspoon pepper

For the Hot Water Crust
3½ cups flour
½ cup cold unsalted
   butter, cubed
1 cup plus
   2 tablespoons water
2 teaspoons salt
¼ cup plus 2 tablespoons
   vegetable shortening
2 eggs
3 drops green gel
   food coloring

Special Tools

2-inch leaf-shaped
   cookie cutter or
   cookie stamp

INSTRUCTIONS

1 Preheat oven to 400°F. Coat two muffin pans with cooking spray and set aside.

2 Combine all the ingredients for the filling in a medium bowl and stir until the garlic is well distributed. Cover with plastic wrap and chill in the refrigerator until ready to use.

3 To make the hot water crust, sift the flour into a large bowl. Rub in the butter until you achieve a texture like bread crumbs.

4 In a small saucepan, bring the water and salt to a boil over medium-high heat, stirring until the salt is dissolved. When the mixture is boiling, add the vegetable shortening and stir until melted. Remove from heat. *To avoid burns, use caution when working with hot fats.*

5 Pour the hot water mix into the flour mix all at once and stir quickly until combined. It will create a shaggy dough. Overturn onto a floured surface and knead until a smooth dough forms. Divide the dough in half, wrap one half in plastic wrap, and set that half aside.

6 Roll the remaining half into a 14" x 19" rectangle approximately ⅛ inch thick. Cut 8 (5-inch) circles from the dough and use them to line the pans, using only every other well to leave adequate space for the pie lids. There should be 6 pies in one pan and 2 in the other. Lightly press any overhang down along the edge of the well.

(Continued on next page)

7 Whisk the eggs together in a bowl and brush the inside and edges of the lined muffin wells (this will seal the dough to help prevent leaks). Evenly distribute the filling among the lined wells (approximately ⅓ cup filling, packed, per pie), packing the filling down tightly to prevent gaps.

8 Unwrap the remaining dough. Re-flour your surface and cut another 8 circles. Use the back of a large piping tip to cut a hole in the center of each circle. Place the circles on top of each pie, crimping the edges to seal. Brush the tops with egg wash.

9 Use the dough scraps to cut out 8 leaves with a 2-inch leaf-shaped cookie cutter or cookie stamp, rerolling the dough if necessary.

10 Whisk the food coloring into your egg wash and dab it onto the leaves with a finger. Gently press the leaves onto the pie lids, making sure they are slightly off-center to avoid covering the hole in the lid.

11 Place the partially filled muffin pan on the top rack in the oven and the full pan on the bottom rack. Bake 40 minutes, swapping the trays halfway through. Allow the pies to rest in the pans for 10 minutes before gently prying them from the pans with a butter knife. To avoid leaks, be careful not to pierce the pies with the knife.

Serve to some dwarves at an unexpected party!

Hobbit Door Giant Chocolate Chip Cookie

Makes 1 (11-inch) chocolate chip cookie

"It had a perfectly round door like a porthole, painted green, with a shiny yellow brass knob in the exact middle."

No matter how you like your chocolate chip cookies, each slice of this sweet treat has something for everyone: a crunchy outer edge, a soft and slightly cakey middle, and a gooey center.

INGREDIENTS

For the Cookie
1½ cups flour
¼ cup malt powder
¾ teaspoon baking soda
1 teaspoon salt
¾ cup butter, softened
6 tablespoons sugar
¼ cup brown sugar, packed
1 teaspoon vanilla extract
2 eggs, room temperature
1½ cups semisweet chocolate chips

For the Frosting
1 cup plus 2 tablespoons butter, softened
4½ cups sifted powdered sugar, divided
2¼ teaspoons vanilla extract
3 tablespoons milk, divided
Green, pastel green, and yellow gel food coloring

Special Tools

Pizza stone

INSTRUCTIONS

1 Sift together the flour, malt powder, baking soda, and salt in a medium bowl. Set aside.

2 In a large bowl, beat together the butter, sugars, and vanilla on medium-low speed until well combined and fluffy. Beat in the eggs one at a time.

3 Gradually beat in the dry mix. Stir in the chocolate chips.

4 Rub a large sheet of plastic wrap with flour. Shape the dough into a 7-inch disk. Wrap the disk in the plastic wrap and chill in the refrigerator for 1 hour.

5 Preheat oven to 375°F. Unwrap the dough and place onto a lightly floured pizza stone. Lightly dust the disk with flour and roll out until it is 2 inches from the edge of the stone. Bake for 20 to 25 minutes or until golden brown and the center feels just set when gently tapped. Remove from oven and allow to rest on the pizza stone for 10 minutes.

6 Slowly slide a knife or large frosting knife under the cookie and gently rotate to separate cookie from stone. Allow to completely cool.

7 To make the frosting, beat the butter in the bowl of a standing mixer on medium speed until smooth. Gradually add 1 cup powdered sugar and beat until combined. Add the vanilla and 1 tablespoon of milk and beat until combined. Alternate beating in the remaining milk and powdered sugar.

(Continued on page 81)

8 Divide the frosting into 3 bowls: $3/4$ cup in one, $1^1/4$ cup in another, and the remainder of the frosting in the last. Mix 9 drops pastel green food coloring in the first bowl, 7 drops green in the second, and 3 to 4 drops yellow in the last.

9 Use a sharp knife to lightly cut an 8-inch circle in the center of the cookie 2 inches from the edge. Spread the pastel green frosting into a flat layer over the circle. This will leave a 2-inch-wide circle of the cookie uncovered with frosting. Transfer the regular green frosting to a piping bag fitted with a large round tip and pipe two concentric circles over the exposed area to cover it. Lightly spread flat with a frosting knife to smooth over the edges. Transfer the remaining regular green frosting to a piping bag fitted with a small round tip and pipe four equidistant vertical lines across the pastel green circle in the center. Transfer the yellow frosting to a piping bag fitted with a small round writing tip. Pipe two large dots of frosting midway down the outer border, directly across from each other. This will separate your two lines of text. Pipe the words "The road goes ever on and on" across the top half of the border and "Down from the door where it began" across the bottom half. You can lightly trace the letters with a toothpick beforehand to be sure you write the letters small enough to fit. Use your remaining yellow frosting to pipe a $1^1/2$-inch circle in the center of the cookie and pipe Gandalf's rune in the lower right-hand corner of the door (it looks like an "F" with the two arms slanted upward).

Serve to a passing wizard . . . be sure to wish him a good morning!

Bag End Orchard Salad

Makes 4 side salads

Just like the pork pies (page 77) in this menu, this salad is inspired by the unexpected party Bilbo hosts for the dwarves. Of course, in true hobbit fashion, he would not have let short notice result in poor hospitality. This perfectly balanced salad has everything you could want in an autumn dish: sweet-tart apples, juicy pears, buttery pine nuts, hearty kale, creamy goat cheese, and succulent pomegranate. And it all comes together in a snap!

INGREDIENTS

For the Salad
¼ cup pine nuts
3 cups kale, torn into
   bite-size pieces and
   lightly packed
½ Bartlett pear
½ Honeycrisp apple
½ pomegranate, seeded*
¼ cup plus 2 tablespoons
   crumbled goat cheese

For the Dressing
2 tablespoons
   pomegranate juice
2 teaspoons lemon juice
1 teaspoon honey
½ teaspoon white
   balsamic vinegar
⅛ teaspoon salt
⅛ teaspoon pepper

INSTRUCTIONS

1 Preheat oven to 325°F. Spread pine nuts evenly on a baking sheet and toast for 5 minutes or until very lightly browned. Set aside.

2 Cut pear into ¼-inch cubes. Cut apple into thin slivers, then cut the slivers in half width-wise.

3 Combine all salad ingredients together in a large bowl and toss to combine.

4 Combine all dressing ingredients in a small sealable container. Secure the lid and vigorously shake the container for 1 to 2 minutes or until ingredients are thoroughly combined.

5 Drizzle dressing over salad and toss to combine.

Serve to a gathering of hungry hobbits and dwarves!

*Pomegranate seeds can burst easily while being removed from the husk, so it is important to work carefully while deseeding to avoid juice stains. However, pre-seeded pomegranate arils can be purchased in the produce section of most grocery stores when in season.

Holiday on the Homestead

The Little House books

By Laura Ingalls Wilder

"The coffee boiled, the cakes baked, the meat fried, and they all smelled so good that Laura grew hungrier and hungrier."

—*Little House on the Prairie*

Menu

Skillet Cornbread with Homemade Butter, 87

Simple Roasted Sweet Potatoes, 89

Venison Pot Roast, 91

Maple Candy, 93

Skillet Cornbread with Homemade Butter

Makes 1 (10-inch) cornbread and 6 ounces butter

"Then she split two cold corn-cakes and spread them with molasses. She gave one to Mary and one to Laura. That was their dinner, and it was very good."
—Little House on the Prairie

No-rise, no-knead breads like cornbread were a dietary staple for pioneers like the Ingalls family. Pair it with some homemade butter, and you have a simple, satisfying side dish perfect for Thanksgiving on the prairie. I highly recommend spreading some honey butter on it while it's still hot, allowing the butter to melt to form a glistening glaze.

INGREDIENTS

For the Butter and Buttermilk
2 cups heavy
   whipping cream
1/8 teaspoon salt
1 tablespoon honey
   (optional)

For the Cornbread
2 tablespoons butter,
   divided (from the
   recipe above)
1 cup flour
1 cup cornmeal
1½ teaspoons
   baking powder
¼ teaspoon baking soda
1¼ teaspoons salt
1½ tablespoons sugar
2 eggs,
   room temperature
1 cup buttermilk, room
   temperature (from the
   recipe above)

INSTRUCTIONS

1 To make the butter and buttermilk, pour the cream into the bowl of standing mixer with a whisk attachment. Gradually bring the mixer to full speed, increasing the speed 2 settings at a time and spending 2 minutes at each new speed. Stop to scrape the sides of the bowl if necessary.

2 Continue to beat the mixture at full speed until it begins to separate into solid clumps of fat (butter) and liquid (buttermilk). It may take up to 4 minutes to reach this stage. You will know you have reached it when you begin to hear a small splashing sound and bits of liquid begin to splatter against the side of the bowl.

3 Reduce the mixer to half speed (or the highest speed that does not result in liquid spraying out of the bowl). Continue to beat for about 1 more minute, reducing speed as needed to prevent spraying. While the beater is going, carefully scrape the sides of the bowl as needed.

4 When most of the butter has separated from the buttermilk and gathered in the center of the whisk, stop the beater and press the butter from the whisk into the bowl with a spatula.

(Continued on next page)

5 Drain the mixer bowl through a colander over a medium bowl to catch the buttermilk. Set the buttermilk out on the counter to use for the cornbread recipe below.

6 Knead and squeeze the butter into a ball until no more buttermilk comes out. Under very cold running water, continue to knead the butter for 3 minutes. Turn off water and knead butter until no more water drips out. Transfer butter to a clean bowl and set aside.

7 Rinse and dry the mixer bowl and whisk attachment. Return the butter to the mixer bowl and beat in the salt and honey (if using). Transfer butter to a small bowl and cover with plastic wrap or a lid to seal. Chill in the refrigerator until ready to use.

8 To make the cornbread, begin by preheating oven to 425°F. Melt 1 tablespoon butter and set aside.

9 In a large bowl, whisk together flour, cornmeal, baking powder, baking soda, salt, and sugar with a fork. Create a well in the center.

10 Whisk the eggs and melted butter into the buttermilk. Pour the buttermilk mix into the well in the center of the bowl and whisk with a fork until just combined. Set aside.

11 Heat the remaining 1 tablespoon of butter in a 11-inch cast-iron skillet on medium-high heat until foaming and the batter sizzles strongly when flicked into the skillet (about 2 minutes). Pour the batter into the skillet all at once and quickly spread it across the bottom of the skillet in an even layer. Allow to cook for 1 minute.

12 Transfer the skillet to the oven and bake for 15 to 20 minutes until bread is golden and springs back when firmly tapped with a finger.

Serve warm at a frontier Thanksgiving!

Simple Roasted Sweet Potatoes

Makes 2½ cups sweet potatoes

"Mr. Edwards was taking sweet potatoes out of his pockets....There were nine sweet potatoes. Mr. Edwards had brought them all the way from town, too....There were the sweet potatoes, baked in the ashes and carefully wiped so that you could eat the good skins, too."
—Little House on the Prairie

Sometimes it's the simplest food preparations that let the ingredients shine. These roasted sweet potatoes are seasoned with just a touch of garlic, thyme, salt, and pepper—embracing the savory side of sweet.

INGREDIENTS

2 medium sweet potatoes (approx. 1 lb.)
2 tablespoons olive oil
1 cloves garlic, minced
1½ teaspoons fresh thyme leaves
½ teaspoon salt
⅛ teaspoon pepper

INSTRUCTIONS

1 Preheat oven to 375°F. Thoroughly rinse and scrub potatoes with clean water and pat dry. Cut into ¾-inch cubes and place in a medium bowl. Add remaining ingredients to the bowl and stir until well combined.

2 Transfer potato mix to an ungreased baking sheet and spread out evenly. Bake for 20 minutes or until fork-tender.

Serve after a long day of traveling across the frontier!

Venison Pot Roast

Makes 1 (3.5-lb.) neck roast with vegetables and 2 cups gravy

"That was a wonderful supper. They sat by the camp fire and ate the tender, savory, flavory meat till they could eat no more. When at last Laura set down her plate, she sighed with contentment. She didn't want anything more in the world."
—Little House on the Prairie

The Ingalls family didn't have a slow cooker, but given venison's reputation for toughness, I decided to turn to modern technology to optimize this recipe. The slow cooker traps moisture and slowly renders fat, easily resulting in a tender, flavorful roast.

INGREDIENTS

2 medium parsnips, peeled and chopped
2 medium carrots, peeled and chopped
1 large yellow onion, peeled and chopped
1 large celery stalk, chopped
1 cup beef broth
2 tablespoons olive oil
3½ lb. venison neck roast (bound into a 4" x 9" log to fit in the slow cooker if necessary)
1 teaspoon kosher salt
½ teaspoon garlic powder
¼ teaspoon pepper
1 bay leaf
1 (7-inch) sprig rosemary
½ cup flour
1 small drizzle browning sauce
Additional salt and pepper to taste, if desired

Special Tools

Slow cooker
Fine-mesh strainer

INSTRUCTIONS

1 Add vegetables and beef broth to a slow cooker.

2 Add oil to a large skillet over medium-high heat and brown venison on all sides. Sprinkle with salt, garlic powder, and pepper. Transfer to the slow cooker. Add the bay and rosemary.

3 Cover and cook on low heat for 6 hours until internal temperature reaches 140°F. Use tongs to transfer roast to a serving plate. Scoop vegetables out of the slow cooker with a slotted spoon and transfer to a serving plate. Cover with aluminum foil to keep warm and set aside. Strain remaining liquid through a fine-mesh strainer into a bowl.

4 Return liquid to the slow cooker and set heat to high. Whisk in flour and browning sauce. Continue whisking for 3 minutes (mixture will thicken considerably). Taste and add additional salt and pepper to taste, if desired (approximately ¼ teaspoon salt and ⅛ teaspoon pepper). Transfer gravy to a serving dish.

5 Remove foil cover from roast and garnish with additional rosemary if desired.

Serve to a family of hungry pioneers!

Maple Candy

Makes 27 pieces

*"One morning she boiled molasses and sugar together until they made
a thick syrup, and Pa brought in two pans of clean, white snow from
outdoors. . . . Pa and Ma showed them how to pour the dark syrup in little
streams onto the snow . . . these hardened at once and were candy."*
—Little House in the Big Woods

These simple pioneer candies are easy to make ahead for your Thanksgiving celebration. Simply leave them in the mold in the refrigerator for up to 5 days before serving.

INGREDIENTS

1½ cups pure
  maple syrup

Special Tools

Candy thermometer
1" x 1" x ½" maple leaf
  candy mold

INSTRUCTIONS

1 Add syrup to a small saucepan over medium-low heat and bring to 280°F on a candy thermometer. Pour into molds and chill for 45 minutes.

2 To serve, place each candy in a square of wax paper, fold down the top and bottom of the square, and twist the ends closed. Place the wrapped candies in a serving bowl.

Serve as a sweet conclusion to a Thanksgiving meal!

An Autumnal Abbey Feast

Redwall

By Brian Jacques

"But the excitement of the feast had gripped Samkin, and he ran to his place
at table . . . as he called out, 'Hey, Mrs. Spinney, are those apple turnovers hot?
Pass me one, will you please. Oho, look at your Great Hall cake, Arula.
It's the best one in all of Mossflower, isn't it, Friar Bellows?"

–Salamandastron, by Brian Jacques and Gary Chalk

Menu

Loamhedge Nutbread, 97

Leek and Potato Soup with Parsnip and Garlic, 99

Deeper 'n Ever Turnip 'n Tater 'n Beetroot Pie, 101

Damson Plum and Pear Crumbles with Meadowcream and Mint, 103

Loamhedge Nutbread

Makes 1 (7-inch) loaf

*"Abruc stood up and stretched. 'Ye may do, Lonna, but Garfo Trok ain't a
beast that's ever stinted 'isself when it comes to vittles, particularly nutbread.
Why that ole dog'd go to Hellgates for a loaf!'"*
—Loamhedge

The secret to this crave-able, satisfying bread? Roasted garlic. Raw garlic will do in a pinch, but roasting it first allows the flavors to deepen and introduces a subtle sweetness. This recipe only uses two cloves, but you can save the rest to spread on toast, mix with mashed potatoes, or even use with other recipes from this book, such as White Whiskey Baked Beans with Bacon (page 65) or Leek and Potato Soup with Parsnip and Garlic (page 99).

INGREDIENTS

1 head garlic (if roasting),
  2 cloves garlic (if not)
1 teaspoon olive oil
2 cups flour
1 teaspoon salt
1 teaspoon baking soda
2 teaspoons
  fresh rosemary,
  finely chopped
½ cup chopped walnuts
1 cup buttermilk

INSTRUCTIONS

1 To roast the garlic, preheat oven to 425°F. Remove most of the outer skin from the garlic head and slice off the top, cutting far enough down that all the cloves are exposed. Drizzle the top with olive oil. Wrap in foil and bake on an ungreased baking sheet for 30 minutes or until golden brown and soft. Use 2 cloves for this recipe.

2 To make the bread, preheat oven to 400°F. Line a baking sheet with parchment paper and set aside. In a large bowl, stir together flour, salt, baking soda, and rosemary. Mince garlic and add to the bowl, rubbing it through the flour mix with your fingers to evenly incorporate. Scatter walnuts across the top of the flour mix but do not stir.

3 Add the buttermilk all at once and stir until just combined. The baking soda reaction begins as soon as the buttermilk is added, so you want to move quickly after the dough has been stirred up.

4 Scrape the dough onto a well-floured surface. Dust hands with flour and sprinkle over dough. Shape the dough into a 7-inch round loaf, working quickly. Transfer loaf to the baking sheet and score a large "X" across the entire top of the loaf with a sharp knife, cutting down until you are about a ¼ inch from the bottom of the loaf. Bake for 35 minutes or until golden and the bottom sounds hollow when firmly tapped with a finger. Transfer to a wire rack to cool.

Serve to some hungry woodland creatures!

Leek and Potato Soup with Parsnip and Garlic

Makes 7 cups

"The Honeysuckle's crew found that the Dunehog hospitality was not lacking. For supper they dined on a fine leek and potato soup, followed by mushroom, radish, and seafood stew, with an enormous fruit trifle for dessert."
—The Legend of Luke

The secret to this rustic yet velvety smooth soup? Cooking the leeks low and slow before adding the vegetable stock. Of course, a generous amount of Parmesan cheese doesn't hurt, either.

INGREDIENTS

3 leeks (14.5 oz.), white and light green portion only and roots cut off
¼ cup butter
2 cloves garlic, minced
3-4 Yukon Gold potatoes (1 lb., 5 oz.)
2 large parsnips (9 oz.)
1 quart vegetable stock
¾ cup whole milk, room temperature
3 ounces Parmesan cheese
½ teaspoon salt
⅛ teaspoon white or black pepper
Spiced pine nuts (page 236) for garnish (optional)
Parsley for garnish (optional)

INSTRUCTIONS

1   Slice leeks in half lengthwise, discarding outer layers if heavily soiled. Slice width-wise into thin strips and place in a colander. Rinse thoroughly under cold water and set aside.

2   Melt butter in a large pot over medium heat. Add leeks and garlic. Cook, stirring regularly, for 3 minutes. Reduce heat to medium-low and cook for 40 minutes, stirring regularly.

3   Peel potatoes and parsnips and cut into ½-inch pieces. Add to the pot, along with the vegetable stock. Bring to a boil on medium-high heat. Reduce heat to medium-low and simmer 20 to 30 minutes until vegetables are very soft.

4   Transfer half of the soup to a blender and blend until smooth. Transfer to a clean bowl and set aside. Blend remaining soup and transfer both halves back to the pot (alternatively, this can all be done in the pot with an immersion blender). Very gradually stir in milk. Grate the Parmesan and stir in until melted. Stir in salt and pepper. Top with spiced pine nuts and sprigs of parsley, if desired.

Serve at an autumn banquet at Redwall Abbey!

Deeper 'n Ever Turnip 'n Tater 'n Beetroot Pie

Makes 1 (9-inch) pie

"There ain't no better cook in all of Mossflower than Friar Wopple. She makes pies an' soups, an' pasties . . . an' deeper 'n ever turnip 'n tater 'n beetroot pie for the moles. Best food you ever tasted."
—Uggo, The Rogue Crew

The ultimate root vegetable dish, this savory pie boasts buttery herbed crust and hearty diced vegetable filling with a flavor reminiscent of Thanksgiving stuffing. Like all the recipes eaten by the beasts of Redwall, it's naturally vegetarian . . . but I won't fault you if you add some diced chicken!

INGREDIENTS

For the Filling
1 cup chopped
    sweet onion
½ cup butternut squash,
    peeled and cubed
1 cup white turnip, peeled
    and cubed
1 cup parsnip, peeled
    and cubed
1 cup carrots, peeled
    and cubed
1 cup beets, peeled
    and cubed
1 cup chopped celery
1 cup sliced mushrooms
3 tablespoons olive oil
½ teaspoon salt
¼ teaspoon pepper

For the Binding Mix
4 red potatoes
2 cloves garlic, minced
½ teaspoon salt
1 tablespoon parsley flakes
1 teaspoon rosemary
1 egg, room temperature

For the Pie Dough
1¼ cups flour
½ teaspoon salt
½ tablespoon dried thyme
½ tablespoon dried rosemary
6 tablespoons cold unsalted butter, cubed
¼ cup cold water

INSTRUCTIONS

1 Preheat oven to 400°F. Combine all the filling ingredients in a large bowl; stir until the vegetables are evenly coated with the olive oil. Line a baking sheet with aluminum foil and evenly spread out the vegetables on it. Roast for 45 minutes, stirring halfway through. At the 15-minute mark, pierce the red potatoes for the binding mix

(Continued on next page)

4 to 5 times with a fork and place them on the baking sheet with the vegetables for the remaining cook time.

2 While you wait, make the pie dough. In a medium bowl, stir together all the pie dough ingredients except the butter and water. Cut the butter into the flour mix with a fork. Stir in water 1 tablespoon at a time until the mix holds together when pressed with fingers but isn't soggy. Gather it into a ball and flatten into a 4$\frac{1}{2}$-inch disk. Wrap the disk in plastic and freeze 15 to 20 minutes or until firm but not hard.

3 Roll the dough out on a floured surface until it reaches 12 inches across (if the dough is still too stiff to roll, work it with your hands until it becomes pliable). Line a pie plate with the dough. Trim the edges and decorate if desired.

4 Remove the vegetables from the oven. Mash the red potatoes in a large bowl and stir in all the other binding mix ingredients. Stir the roasted vegetables into the binding mix 1 cup at a time. Pour mix into pie crust.

5 Bake 15 minutes at 400°F. Turn the oven down to 350°F and bake another 25 to 30 minutes or until the crust and top of the pie begin to lightly brown.

Slice and serve warm to the wonderful beasts of Redwall!

Damson Plum and Pear Crumbles with Meadowcream and Mint

Makes 1 9" x 13" pan (approximately 8 servings)

"There was bread and cheese aplenty at the dinner table, with some tasty vegetable soup, a selection of pasties, a fine summer salad, plus damson and pear crumble for dessert, with the option of a honeyed plum pudding."
—Doomwyte

Damson plums can be difficult to find in most major chain grocery stores even while in season, so this recipe uses damson preserves—much more widely available throughout the year! Just be aware that some brands carry a warning that the preserves may contain pits. Damson pits are notoriously difficult to remove from the raw fruit, so jam-makers often strain them from the prepared preserves. This carries the risk of missing a few, so keep an eye out for them while whisking the preserves in this recipe.

INGREDIENTS

For the Plum and Pear Crumble
4½ lb. ripe pears
1 cup damson plum preserves
3 tablespoons cornstarch
2 teaspoons lemon juice
½ teaspoon salt
½ cup rolled oats
½ cup brown sugar, packed
¼ cup flour
½ teaspoon cinnamon
½ teaspoon nutmeg
¼ teaspoon cloves
¼ cup unsalted butter, cold
½ cup chopped pecans

For the Meadowcream
1½ cups heavy cream
3 tablespoons honey
Mint leaves, for garnish

INSTRUCTIONS

1 To make the plum and pear crumble, preheat oven to 350°F. Peel, quarter, and core the pears. Cut into ½-inch wedges (approximately 3 wedges per quarter). Add to a large pot.

2 In a medium bowl, thoroughly whisk together the preserves, cornstarch, lemon juice, and salt. Add to the pot and stir until well combined.

3 Place pot over medium-high heat and cook for 20 to 25 minutes, stirring regularly. The juices should be thickened and the pears soft but not mushy.

4 Transfer mix to a 9" x 13" glass baking pan. In a medium bowl, add the oats, brown sugar, flour, cinnamon, nutmeg, and cloves. Stir with a fork until well combined. Cut the butter into cubes and rub into the oat mix until it has a texture like bread crumbs. Stir in the pecans. Sprinkle evenly over pear mix.

5 Bake for 20 minutes until top is baked through and the pear mix is bubbling. Remove from oven and allow to rest for at least 10 minutes.

(Continued on page 105)

6 To make the meadowcream, beat heavy cream in the bowl of a standing mixer on medium-high speed for a few minutes until it begins to have a solid texture but does not yet form peaks. Stop the mixer. Drizzle in the honey and gently stir a few times to keep it from settling to the bottom. Restart mixer and beat until stiff peaks form.

7 Spoon crumble into small bowls and top with meadowcream and sprigs of mint.

Serve to celebrate a good harvest!

Note: This recipe is especially good à la mode!

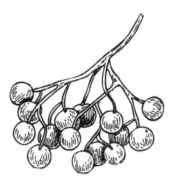

Dinner at the Van Tassel Mansion

"The Legend of Sleepy Hollow"
By Washington Irving

"Fain would I pause to dwell upon the world of charms that burst upon the enraptured gaze of my hero, as he entered the state parlor of Van Tassel's mansion . . . the ample charms of a genuine Dutch country tea-table, in the sumptuous time of autumn."

Menu
Apple Cider Crullers, 109

Brown Sugar Glazed Turkey, 111

Smashed Pumpkin Soup, 113

Maple Walnut Apple Pie, 115

Apple Cider Crullers

Makes approximately 24 crullers

"Such heaped up platters of cakes of various and almost indescribable kinds, known only to experienced Dutch housewives! There was the doughty doughnut, the tender oly koek, and the crisp and crumbling cruller."

These French-style crullers use choux pastry as a base instead of traditional doughnut dough, resulting in a doughnut that is crisp on the outside and almost custardy on the inside.

INGREDIENTS

For the Crullers
½ cup butter
½ cup water
½ cup apple cider
1 cup flour
4 eggs,
  thoroughly beaten
Vegetable oil, for frying
  (approximately 8 cups,
  depending on the size
  of the pot)

For the Icing
1 cup powdered sugar,
  sifted
2 tablespoons
  apple cider

Special Tools

Candy thermometer
Metal tongs

Serve at a party at the Van Tassel mansion!

INSTRUCTIONS

1 Cut a sheet of parchment paper into 24 (3-inch) squares and set aside. Place a wire rack over a baking sheet and set aside.

2 Melt the butter, water, and cider together in a medium saucepan on low heat. Turn the heat to medium and bring to a boil. Turn off the heat and pour in the flour all at once. Stir together quickly with a silicone spatula. Turn the heat back to medium. Cook for 2 minutes, stirring constantly. Remove from heat. With a hand mixer on medium speed, beat the eggs into the saucepan of dough ½ tablespoon at a time until smooth.

3 Fit a piping bag with a jumbo star tip and fill the bag half full with dough (the density of choux pastry makes it easier to pipe a ½ batch at a time).

4 Fill a large pot at least 3 inches deep with vegetable oil and place over medium heat. Allow the oil to come to 350°F.

5 While you wait, pipe a 2½-inch circle of dough onto each of your parchment squares. When you run out of dough, refill the bag and continue piping

6 Gently lower 2 to 3 crullers into the oil, parchment-side-down. After about 10 to 15 seconds, you should be able to easily pull the parchment squares out of the oil with a pair of metal tongs. Discard the parchment. Fry the crullers for about 2 minutes on each side until they are a strong golden-brown color. Gently remove them from the oil with metal tongs and place on the prepared rack and baking sheet to drain. Repeat with remaining crullers.

7 While the crullers fry, stir together the icing ingredients until smooth. When all the crullers are finished, drizzle on the icing.

Brown Sugar Glazed Turkey

Makes 1 (15-lb.) turkey

"The pedagogue's mouth watered as he looked upon this sumptuous promise of luxurious winter fare . . . not a turkey but he beheld daintily trussed up, with its gizzard under its wing."

This recipe is a great option for beginners who are ready to try their hand at roasting a large bird for the first time. No need to worry about brining, basting, trussing, or complicated stuffing. A simple pre-salting stage helps ensure crispy skin, while the phenomenal brown sugar glaze elevates a plain old turkey to something special without added difficulty.

INGREDIENTS

For the Turkey
1 (15-lb.) turkey (thawed if frozen, giblets and neck removed)
3 tablespoons kosher salt, divided
1 teaspoon black pepper
3 tablespoons olive oil
1 orange, quartered
2 large sprigs rosemary
1 cup cranberries

For the Glaze
1 cup apple cider
½ cup brown sugar, packed
1 teaspoon lemon juice
¼ teaspoon ground ginger
¼ teaspoon kosher salt
⅛ teaspoon pepper

Special Tools
13" x 18" baking sheet

INSTRUCTIONS

1 Pat the turkey dry with a paper towel and rub the entire exterior with 2 tablespoons salt and the pepper. Line a 13" x 18" baking sheet with aluminum foil and place a wire rack on top. Place turkey on the wire rack and chill, uncovered, in the refrigerator for 10 hours.

2 Place oven racks in the top and bottom positions in the oven. Preheat oven to 350°F.

3 Rub the turkey with olive oil, making sure to separate the skin from the breast meat by sliding your fingers underneath and oiling there as well. Rub with remaining 1 tablespoon of salt.

4 Fill the cavity of the bird with the orange, rosemary, and cranberries. Do not truss the legs (this will help the turkey cook more evenly). Tuck the tips of the wings underneath the turkey. Cook for 2 hours.

5 While you wait, prepare the glaze. Combine all the glaze ingredients in a small saucepan and stir until sugar is dissolved. Bring to a boil over medium heat. Reduce heat to medium-low and simmer for 15 minutes. Set aside.

6 When the 2 hours are up, increase the heat to 425°F and brush the turkey with glaze every 15 minutes. Continue to cook for 1 hour or until the internal temperature reaches 150°F. Allow turkey to rest for 30 minutes before carving.

Serve at a feast in Sleepy Hollow!

Note: You need to chill the turkey for 10 hours in Step 1 before you can proceed with the rest of the recipe.

Smashed Pumpkin Soup

Makes 6½ cups pumpkin soup

"In one part of the road leading to the church was found the saddle trampled in the dirt; the tracks of horses' hoofs deeply dented in the road, and evidently at furious speed, were traced to the bridge, beyond which . . .was found the hat of the unfortunate Ichabod, and close beside it a shattered pumpkin."

No Thanksgiving is complete without a pumpkin dish, and pumpkin soup is a hassle-free way to scratch that itch. This iteration includes bacon for added salt and substance.

INGREDIENTS

1 sweet potato
   (approximately 1 lb.)
2 large carrots
1 sweet onion
1 tablespoon olive oil
½ teaspoon rosemary
1 teaspoon salt
¼ teaspoon pepper
12 slices bacon
1 (15-oz.) can
   pumpkin puree
2½ cups vegetable stock
Sour cream, for garnish
Snipped green onion,
   for garnish

INSTRUCTIONS

1 Preheat oven to 400°F. Peel and cut sweet potato, carrots, and onion into ½-inch pieces. Place in a large bowl with the olive oil, rosemary, salt, and pepper. Stir until evenly coated. Spread the vegetable mix out evenly on a baking sheet and bake for 20 minutes or until fork tender, stirring halfway through.

2 While the vegetables cook, cut the bacon into bits and fry, transferring to a paper-towel-lined plate to drain. Set ⅓ of the bacon bits aside for garnish.

3 Place half of all ingredients except garnishes (vegetables, remaining bacon bits, pumpkin, and stock) in a blender and blend until smooth. Transfer to a large pot.

4 Repeat Step 3 with remaining half of ingredients. Place over medium heat until heated through, stirring occasionally.

5 Ladle into bowls and top with sour cream, snipped green onion, and reserved bacon bits.

Serve in the pumpkin head of a ghostly horseman!

Maple Walnut Apple Pie

Makes 1 (9-inch) pie

"Such heaped up platters of cakes of various and almost indescribable kinds, known only to experienced Dutch housewives. . . . And then there were apple pies, and peach pies, and pumpkin pies. . . . Happily, Ichabod Crane was not in so great a hurry as his historian, but did ample justice to every dainty."

This pie may look elaborate, but the striking visual effect of the top crust is achieved by simply arranging shapes cut with cookie stamps (or cookie cutters, if you don't have stamps) into concentric circles.

INGREDIENTS

For the Crust
2½ cups flour
½ cup ground walnuts
1 teaspoon salt
¾ cup cold unsalted butter, cubed
½ cup cold water, plus more if necessary
1 egg mixed with 1 tablespoon water, for egg wash
½ tablespoon turbinado sugar, for sprinkling

For the Filling
3 Pink Lady apples
2 Granny Smith apples
½ cup pure maple syrup
1 tablespoon flour
¾ teaspoon cinnamon
¼ teaspoon salt
2 tablespoons cold unsalted butter, cubed

Special Tools
2-inch maple leaf cookie cutter or cookie stamp
1½-inch apple cookie cutter or cookie stamp

INSTRUCTIONS

1 In a large bowl, stir together flour, walnuts, and salt. Add the butter and work through with fingers or a fork until the butter is evenly distributed and in pea-sized pieces.

2 Drizzle in ¼ cup cold water and work through with a fork. Continue adding water 1 tablespoon at a time until the dough holds together when pressed with fingers and is damp but not wet. Shape dough into 2 equal balls and flatten into 4-inch disks. Wrap tightly in plastic wrap and chill in the refrigerator for 45 to 60 minutes until firm but not hard.

3 While the dough chills, start the filling. Peel, core, and cut apples into ¼-inch-thick slices. Place in a large bowl.

4 Whisk together the maple syrup and flour with a fork until well combined. Add to the bowl along with the cinnamon and salt. Stir well to combine. Cover with plastic wrap and set aside.

5 Preheat oven to 425°F. When the dough has chilled, unwrap the first disk and roll it out on a lightly floured surface until it reaches 14 inches across, reflouring surface and rolling pin as needed to prevent sticking. Transfer to a 9-inch pie pan and trim the edges to fit.

6 Give the filling a good stir, making sure to scrape the bottom to incorporate as much of the syrup mix as possible (it acts as a thickener). Lay apple pieces in layers along the bottom of the pie pan.* Drizzle a few large spoonfuls

(Continued on next page)

of remaining liquid over the top. Scatter the cubed butter across the top.

7 Re-flour work surface and pin and roll the second disk of dough until it reaches 14 inches across. Use cookie cutters and/or cookie stamps to cut out 41 (2-inch) maple leaves and 1 (1½-inch) apple. Arrange leaves on the pie so they slightly overlap and are in concentric circles. Be sure to lay the first circle inside the pie pan and not on the outer crust of the pie, so that a narrow band around the outer edge is left uncovered (this will act as a vent to allow steam to escape). Place the apple-shaped cutout in the center of the pie.

8 Brush with egg wash and sprinkle with turbinado sugar. Bake for 45 to 50 minutes or until the crust is golden brown and the apples inside are tender. When there are only 20 minutes left in the bake time, check the pie for browning. If the crust is as dark as desired, loosely cover the edges of the pie with aluminum foil for the remainder of the bake time. If a darker color is desired, leave uncovered until that color is reached.

9 Remove from oven and allow to rest for 4 to 24 hours.**

Serve at an autumnal feast in Sleepy Hollow!

*Laying individual apple pieces in the pie pan takes longer than dumping them all in at once, but you'll thank yourself later. It helps prevent gaps and encourages even baking.

**This recipe needs at least 4 hours to rest, so be sure to leave plenty of time.

Infused Honey, page 241

A Hundred Acre Celebration

Winnie-the-Pooh

By A. A. Milne

"'Well,' said Pooh, 'what I like best,' and then he had to stop and think. Because although Eating Honey was a very good thing to do, there was a moment just before you began to eat it which was better than when you were, but he didn't know what it was called."

—*The House at Pooh Corner*

Menu

Haycorns, 121

Cottleston Pie, 123

Rabbit's Autumn Harvest Salad, 125

Pooh's Honey Lemon Cookies, 127

Haycorns

Makes 15 haycorns

"I'm planting a haycorn, Pooh, so that it can grow up into an oak-tree, and have lots of haycorns just outside the front door instead of having to walk miles and miles. Do you see, Pooh?"
—*Piglet*, Winnie-the-Pooh

Piglet is one of my favorite fictional characters because he shows that greatness can come in a tiny package. Let's show our appreciation for Piglet by making his favorite food: haycorns! Of course, actual acorns aren't that palatable, but these cheese-based reproductions are just the thing to start a culinary journey through the Hundred Acre Wood.

INGREDIENTS

3 ounces Asiago cheese
4 spreadable Swiss cheese wedges (0.75 oz. each)
¼ cup sliced almonds

INSTRUCTIONS

1 Finely shred the Asiago. In a medium bowl, mix the Asiago and cheese wedges until well combined. Cover and chill in the refrigerator for 30 minutes.

2 Preheat oven to 325°F. Spread the almonds out on an ungreased baking sheet and toast for 3 to 5 minutes or until just slightly brown. Allow to cool, then gather them together in the middle of the pan and finely crush with a rolling pin. Set aside.

3 Line a baking sheet with parchment or wax paper. Scoop the cheese mix into a piping bag fitted with a large round tip. Using a spiral motion, pipe the mix into small cone shapes on the parchment (approximately ½ tablespoon mix per cone). Smooth them with your finger using a downward swiping motion and pinch the tip to get the desired acorn shape.

4 Lightly drape with plastic wrap and chill in the refrigerator for another 30 minutes.

5 Roll the bottoms in crushed almonds to make the acorn cap. Make sure the bottoms are thoroughly coated, since this is what keeps the haycorns from sticking to the serving plate.

Serve while spending time with your favorite Very Small Animal!

Cottleston Pie

Makes 1 (9-inch) potpie

"Cottleston, Cottleston, Cottleston Pie,
A fly can't bird, but a bird can fly.
Ask me a riddle and I reply
Cottleston, Cottleston, Cottleston Pie!"
—Winnie-the-Pooh

Pot pie may not be the first thing you think of when you imagine a Thanksgiving meal, but it's a wonderful way to feed a crowd without having to spend an entire afternoon roasting a turkey. It's also a clever way to use up Thanksgiving leftovers—just swap the chicken for shredded turkey!

INGREDIENTS

1 lb. chicken breast
    tenderloin strips
Olive oil, for brushing
1½ teaspoons salt, divided
¼ teaspoon pepper,
    divided
4 large carrots,
    peeled and cut into
    ½-inch pieces
3 medium red potatoes,
    cut into ½-inch cubes
2 celery stalks, chopped
1 yellow onion, peeled
    and diced
1 cup frozen peas
2 cloves garlic, minced
1 teaspoon dried thyme
1 can cream of
    chicken soup
1 sheet frozen puff
    pastry, thawed
1 egg
1 tablespoon water

Special Tools

Autumn-themed cookie
    cutters (acorn, leaf,
    etc.)

INSTRUCTIONS

1 Preheat oven to 350°F. Evenly space chicken tenderloin strips on a greased baking sheet. Lightly brush with olive oil and season with ½ teaspoon salt and ⅛ teaspoon pepper. Bake for 15 minutes or until juices run clear when chicken is cut.

2 Add the carrots, potatoes, celery, onion, peas, garlic, thyme, soup, and remaining salt and pepper to a large bowl. Cut the chicken into 1-inch pieces and add to bowl. Stir until thoroughly combined.

3 Roll out puff pastry sheet on a lightly floured surface until it creates a 10-inch square. Place a 9-inch 2½-quart oven-safe bowl upside down over the puff pastry and cut around the edge of the bowl. Remove the bowl and transfer the filling to it.

4 Use the back end of a large piping tip (or an apple corer) to cut a hole in the center of the pastry circle. Place the pastry circle over the filling in the oven-safe bowl.

5 Whisk together the egg and water and brush over the pastry. Use autumn-themed cookie cutters to cut out decorative shapes using the dough scraps. Place them on the pastry circle and brush with the egg wash.

6 Place on a baking sheet and bake for 90 minutes. Lightly tent the puff pastry with aluminum foil and bake for another 30 minutes or until filling is cooked through.

7 Allow to rest for at least 10 minutes before serving.

Serve at an autumn party in the Hundred Acre Wood!

Rabbit's Autumn Harvest Salad

Makes 6 servings

"It was going to be one of Rabbit's busy days. As soon as he woke up he felt important, as if everything depended upon him. It was just the day for Organizing Something, or for Writing a Notice Signed Rabbit, or for seeing What Everybody Else Thought About It."
—The House at Pooh Corner

Since this is a Winnie-the-Pooh recipe, it felt appropriate to sweeten this tribute to Rabbit's garden with a touch of honey. However, maple syrup is a delicious, seasonally appropriate alternative.

INGREDIENTS

For the Salad
1 acorn squash (approx. 1 lb., 5 oz.)
2 beets
2 tablespoons olive oil
1 tablespoon honey
1 teaspoon kosher salt
¼ teaspoon pepper
12 large turnip greens, deveined*
6 large basil leaves
¾ cup chopped walnuts, toasted if desired
¾ cup crumbled feta cheese
6 tablespoons dried cherries

For the Honey Balsamic Vinaigrette
2 tablespoons balsamic vinegar
2 tablespoons olive oil
1 tablespoon honey
⅛ teaspoon salt
⅛ teaspoon pepper

INSTRUCTIONS

1 Preheat oven to 400°F. Grease 2 baking sheets and set aside.

2 Cut acorn squash in half lengthwise, scoop out seeds with a spoon, and discard seeds. Cut squash halves in half width-wise to create 4 quarters. Cut quarters into ½-inch-thick strips. Transfer to a large bowl.

3 Peel beets and cut into ¼-inch-thick disks. Cut disks in half width-wise and add to bowl, along with olive oil, honey, salt, and pepper. Stir until well coated. Spread out the contents of the bowl on the baking sheets in a single layer. Cook for 20 minutes, flipping and rotating pans halfway through. Remove from oven and allow to cool on the pan for 10 minutes.

4 Cut the turnip greens into bite-size pieces and add to a large serving bowl. Stack the basil leaves on top of each other, roll lengthwise into a tight tube, and cut width-wise into thin strips. Add sliced basil to bowl, along with walnuts, feta cheese, and dried cherries. Add acorn squash and beets and set aside.

5 To make the vinaigrette, add all the vinaigrette ingredients to a small, sealable container such as a mason jar. Seal container and shake for 30 seconds or until well combined. Drizzle dressing over salad and toss to combine.

Serve to your friends in the Hundred Acre Wood!

*Not a fan of turnips? Not to worry. Turnip greens taste nothing like turnip root, and in fact they have a mild but hearty vegetal flavor, similar to kale.

Pooh's Honey Lemon Cookies

Makes 20 cookies

"'I generally have a small something about now . . .' and [Pooh] looked wistfully at the cupboard in the corner of Owl's parlour, 'just a mouthful of condensed milk or whatnot, with perhaps a lick of honey.'"
—Winnie-the-Pooh

A Winnie-the-Pooh menu would not be complete without a tribute to Pooh's favorite snack: honey! These delicate butter cookies are a sweet conclusion to a Hundred Acre feast.

INGREDIENTS

For the Cookies
1 cup flour
1/8 teaspoon
   baking powder
1/2 cup butter, softened
2 tablespoons
   granulated sugar
1/4 cup powdered sugar
1/4 teaspoon salt
1 1/2 teaspoons lemon zest
1 tablespoon honey
2 teaspoons fresh
   lemon juice

For the Icing
1/4 cup powdered sugar
1 1/2 teaspoons honey
3/4 teaspoon lemon juice
Honeycomb candy,
   crushed (optional, see
   page 240)

*Serve to your favorite silly
old bear!*

INSTRUCTIONS

1 To make the cookies, whisk together the flour and baking powder in a small bowl with a fork. Set aside.

2 In an electric mixer on medium-high speed, cream the butter, granulated sugar, powdered sugar, salt, and lemon zest until smooth. Beat in the honey and lemon juice, stopping to scrape the sides of the bowl if necessary. Beat in the flour mix until fully combined.

3 Shape the dough into a 9-inch log and wrap tightly in plastic wrap. Freeze for 25 minutes. Preheat oven to 400°F.

4 Slice half the log into disks that are a little under 1/2-inch thick.

5 Place 12 of the disks 2 inches apart on an ungreased baking sheet and bake for 8 to 10 minutes or until the cookies are set and have just a touch of brown along the edges. While the first batch bakes, rewrap the remainder of the log in plastic wrap and chill in the refrigerator until ready to begin the second batch.

6 Allow the finished cookies to cool for 5 minutes on the baking sheet. Transfer to a wire rack to cool completely.

7 Cut, bake, and cool the remaining half of the log.

8 To make the icing, stir together the powdered sugar, honey, and lemon juice in a small bowl until the mixture is smooth and reaches drizzling consistency. Drizzle the icing over the cookies. If adding honeycomb candy, wait to make and add the icing until just before serving, then sprinkle approximately 1/4 teaspoon crushed honeycomb candy on top of each cookie (it's best to save this for the last minute because the candy can soften if allowed to sit in the open air for too long).

All Hallows' Eve: a time for spooks and sprites, for ghouls and fiends; when wolfmen howl in the distant fog and vampires prowl in search of their next victim. A time when memento mori is on our minds in earnest.

The drama of this season has captured the imagination of writers for centuries—so much so that many authors have become synonymous with Halloween, even if their work predates its celebration as an official holiday. Bram Stoker's *Dracula* brings terrifying ancient legends to the doorstep of the everyday world; Edgar Allan Poe invites us to relish the evocative style of Gothic horror; and Sir Arthur Conan Doyle analyzes the duality of life and death under the scientific lens of a magnifying glass.

Don't let such rich literary tradition go to waste! Halloween parties and literary themes make a perfect pair, so throw on your best red velvet cape and fire up the oven—the night won't last forever!

A Few Quick Bites

Dracula

By Bram Stoker

"Welcome to my house! Come freely. Go safely; and leave something of the happiness you bring."

Menu
Renfield's Spider Chips and Salsa, 133
Robber "Stakes," 135
Dracula's Dinner Rolls, 137
Monstrous Moon Pies, 139

Renfield's Spider Chips and Salsa

Makes 20 spider chips and 3 cups salsa

"[Renfield's] spiders are now becoming as great a nuisance as his flies, and to-day I told him that he must get rid of them . . . when a horrid blow-fly . . . buzzed into the room, he caught it . . . and, before I knew what he was going to do, put it in his mouth and ate it."

This Romanian-inspired take on chips and salsa features blackened bell peppers and paprika for a Central European feel.

INGREDIENTS

For the Salsa
1 green bell pepper, seeded, deveined, and quartered
1 red bell pepper, seeded, deveined, and quartered
4 Roma tomatoes, seeded and diced
½ cup white onion, diced
1 garlic clove, minced
2 teaspoons lime juice
2 teaspoons snipped fresh cilantro
½ teaspoon kosher salt
¼ teaspoon smoked paprika
¼ teaspoon crushed red pepper flakes (optional)

For the Spider Chips
10 (6-inch) blue corn tortillas*
2 tablespoons olive oil
½ tablespoon kosher salt

Special Tools
3-inch spider cookie cutter

INSTRUCTIONS

1 To make the salsa, place an iron skillet over high heat. When pan is very hot, add peppers, blackening for 6 minutes on each side, pressing down on the pieces occasionally to produce an even char.

2 Remove peppers from skillet and allow to cool. Dice and add to a medium bowl with all remaining salsa ingredients. Stir and cover. Allow to marinate for 1 hour.

3 To make the chips, begin by preheating oven to 350°F. Cut 2 spiders from each tortilla.** Place spiders on 2 ungreased baking sheets. Lightly brush both sides with olive oil and sprinkle with kosher salt (there will most likely be oil and salt left over). Bake for 10 to 12 minutes, swapping and rotating the pans halfway through. Transfer to a wire rack to cool.

Serve to a sinister count in the dark dining hall of a decrepit Transylvanian castle!

*Blue corn tortillas can be difficult to find at standard chain grocery stores but are carried at most international markets and Hispanic grocery stores.

**To avoid waste, you can oil, salt, and bake the tortilla scraps into irregular chips for snacking. You can also cut them into thin strips just before baking to add to salads.

Robber "Stakes"

Makes 6 kebabs

"I dined on what they called 'robber steak'—bits of bacon, onion, and beef, seasoned with red pepper, and strung on sticks, and roasted over the fire, in simple style of the London cat's meat!"

These smoky, spicy, slightly sweet kabobs have everything you need in a Halloween party snack, including a little garlic to ward off vampires!

INGREDIENTS

For the Seasoning
1 tablespoon smoked paprika
1 teaspoon salt
¾ teaspoon garlic powder
½ teaspoon crushed red pepper
¼ teaspoon ground mustard
⅛ teaspoon black pepper

For the Kabobs
6 strips thick-cut bacon
10.5 ounces sirloin steak
1 red bell pepper
1 green bell pepper
½ sweet onion
3 tablespoons olive oil

Special Tools

6 kebab skewers
Grill pan

Tip: "The kebabs pictured use metal skewers, but if using wooden or bamboo skewers, be sure to soak them for at least 20 minutes before assembly to avoid scorching."

INSTRUCTIONS

1 Mix together all the seasoning ingredients in a small bowl.

2 To make the kebabs, sprinkle each slice of bacon with approximately ⅛ teaspoon seasoning per side, rubbing gently to adhere. Set aside.

3 Cut steak and bell peppers into 1½-inch pieces and add to a medium-size bowl. Cut onion in half width-wise and separate layers into pieces. Add these to the bowl along with the olive oil. Toss to combine. Sprinkle in half remaining seasoning and stir until well combined. Add remaining seasoning and stir.

4 To assemble the kebabs, take one skewer and push a piece of green pepper about 1 inch down onto the skewer. Next, push the end of a strip of bacon onto the skewer. Add an onion, a red pepper, and a second onion. Push everything down 1 inch farther on the skewer and fold the bacon over the top of the second onion. Skewer that part of the bacon into place. Add a piece of steak and skewer another fold of bacon over that as well. Repeat the process until you have used 4 peppers, 4 onions, and 2 steak cubes. The bacon should be threaded through the other ingredients in a wave pattern. Use this same process to assemble the 5 remaining kebabs.

5 Cook on a hot grill pan for 2 minutes on the wide sides and 1 minute on the narrow sides.

Serve while traveling the Transylvanian countryside in search of an ancient vampire!

Dracula's Dinner Rolls

Makes 15 garlic knots

"Somehow, I do not dread being alone to-night, and I can go to sleep without fear. I shall not mind any flapping outside the window. . . . I never liked garlic before, but to-night it is delightful!"
—Lucy

Don't worry—these buns don't bite! However, if you're a vampire you may find them quite repulsive, since they're packed with seven cloves of garlic!

INGREDIENTS

For the Red Dough
2 tablespoons very warm
  water (not hot)
¼ cup milk,
  room temperature
½ (3½ g) packet active
  dry yeast (approx.
  1⅛ teaspoons)
2 tablespoons butter,
  softened
½ egg
¼ teaspoon salt
3 cloves garlic, minced
2 tablespoons sugar
¼ teaspoon red gel
  food coloring
1¼ cups plus
  2 tablespoons flour

For the Black Dough
2 tablespoons very warm
  water (not hot)
¼ cup milk,
  room temperature
½ (3½ g) packet active
  dry yeast (approx.
  1⅛ teaspoons)
2 tablespoons butter,
  softened
½ egg

¼ teaspoon salt
3 cloves garlic, minced
2 tablespoons sugar
¼ teaspoon black gel food coloring
1¼ cups plus 2 tablespoons flour

For the Glaze
¼ cup butter, softened
1 clove garlic, minced
3¾ teaspoons grated Parmesan cheese

INSTRUCTIONS

1 To make the red buns, first stir together the water and milk in the bowl of a standing mixer. Sprinkle the yeast on top and allow to rest for 5 minutes, stirring gently after 1 to 2 minutes.

2 Add the butter, egg, salt, garlic, sugar, and food coloring to the bowl. Beat on medium-low speed with a paddle attachment for 30 seconds or until the butter is broken up into pieces. Gradually beat in the flour on medium speed until just combined.

3 Turn the dough out onto a floured surface and knead until it is soft, mostly smooth, and only slightly sticky (approximately 5 to 8 minutes). You may need to periodically re-flour the surface to keep the dough from sticking.

4 Coat a large bowl with cooking spray and place the dough inside, turning once to coat. Cover the bowl with a

(Continued on next page)

clean kitchen cloth and allow to rise for 1 hour or until the dough has roughly doubled in size.

5 Repeat Steps 1 to 4 for the black dough.

6 Line two baking sheets with silicone mats or parchment paper. Punch down the red dough. Separate the dough into 15 balls of equal size (approximately 0.8 ounce each) and roll into 5-inch logs.

7 Repeat with the black dough. Line each black log against 1 red log so that they are touching, creating 15 pairs of logs.*

8 Take 1 pair and gently twist it into a spiral log. Pull the log gently until it is approximately 2 to 3 inches longer and tie into a knot by crossing the 2 strands, tucking 1 end through the loop (don't pull it—only tuck), and tucking the other end under the knot.

9 Repeat with all remaining pairs, placing them an equal distance apart on the baking sheets. Cover and allow to rise for another 45 minutes. Preheat oven to 350°F.

10 Bake for 15 minutes, flipping and rotating the pans halfway through. Allow to cool for 5 minutes on the baking sheet.

11 For the glaze, place butter and garlic in a small microwave-safe bowl. Microwave on high until butter is melted, approximately 30 seconds. Stir to evenly disperse garlic. Brush rolls with melted butter mix and sprinkle 1/4 teaspoon Parmesan on each bun.

Serve warm to your friends to protect them from vampires!

*The prep and rise times for each dough should line up so that the black dough is ready to be punched down by the time the red dough has been separated and rolled.

Monstrous Moon Pies

Makes 16 mini moon pies

"Just then the moon, sailing through the black clouds, appeared behind the jagged crest of a beetling, pine-clad rock, and by its light I saw around us a ring of wolves, with white teeth and lolling red tongues, with long, sinewy limbs and shaggy hair."

The moon pies pictured here are decorated with a vampire motif, but feel free to get creative. You can take your inspiration from *Frankenstein*, *The Wolfman*, or even *Jekyll and Hyde*!

INGREDIENTS

16 graham crackers
1 batch homemade
    marshmallows, cut
    into 2-inch circles (see
    page 239)
2 lb. white almond bark
¾ cup butter, softened
3 cups powdered sugar,
    sifted
1½ teaspoons
    vanilla extract
3 tablespoons milk
Red gel icing,
    store-bought*
Blue gel food coloring
Purple gel food coloring
Black gel food coloring
Yellow gel food coloring

Special Tools

2-inch round
    cookie cutter

INSTRUCTIONS

1 Line a baking sheet with wax paper and set aside. Break the graham crackers in half and cut each half into a circle using a 2-inch round cookie cutter. Place each marshmallow between 2 graham cracker rounds.**

2 Melt half the almond bark according to package instructions and transfer to a large mug or glass measuring cup. Lower each graham sandwich until completely submerged, lifting it out with a fork and gently tapping the fork over the cup for 10 seconds or so to catch drips. Place on the wax paper-lined baking sheet and allow to rest for 20 minutes or until set. When the bark gets too shallow for dipping, melt and use the remaining half.

3 To make the frosting, beat the butter in the bowl of a standing mixer on medium speed until fluffy. Sift in 1 cup powdered sugar and beat until smooth. Beat in vanilla and 1 tablespoon milk until combined. Alternate beating in remaining powdered sugar and milk. Divide frosting between 4 bowls: 3 tablespoons in 2 of the bowls and ¼ cup plus 1 tablespoon in the remaining 2 bowls. Stir 2 drops blue gel food coloring into one of the large portions and 2 drops purple into the other large portion. In the bowls with the smaller portions, stir 3 drops black gel coloring in one and 1 drop yellow in the other.

4 Transfer the blue and purple frosting to piping bags fitted with medium star piping tips (such as Wilton #30 or #21 tips). Transfer the black and yellow to bags with small round writing tips (such as Wilton #2 or #4 tips).

(Continued on page 141)

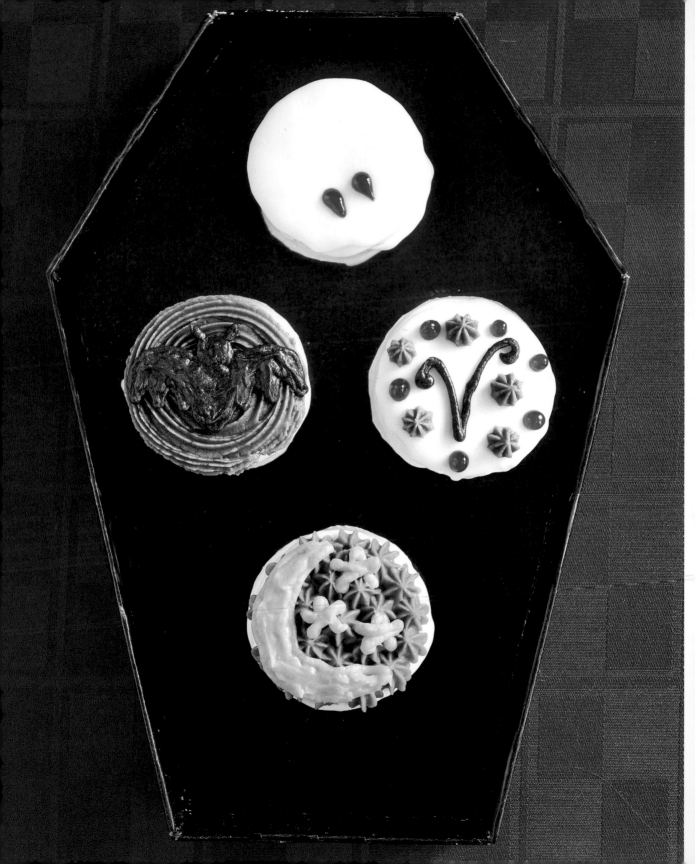

5 Pipe blue frosting over the top of 4 moon pies, then use the yellow frosting to add moons and stars. Pipe purple frosting over the top of 4 moon pies, then use the black frosting to add bats. Pipe a black letter "V" over 4 moon pies and surround it with purple and red dots (use the red gel icing to create the red dots). On the 4 remaining moon pies, pipe 2 dots of red gel icing. Drag the tip of a toothpick through each dot to create the appearance of bite marks.

Serve to guests of your ancient castle to distract them from your vampiric tendencies!

*This can be found in the baking section of most grocery stores.

**No waste needed here! Save the graham cracker and marshmallow scraps to use on top of ice cream, chocolate pudding, mousse, or frosted brownies.

Once upon a Midnight Party

Complete Tales & Poems

By Edgar Allan Poe

"While I nodded, nearly napping, suddenly there came a tapping,
As of some one gently rapping, rapping at my chamber door.
'Tis some visitor,' I muttered, 'tapping at my chamber door —'"

—"The Raven"

Menu

Deviled Raven Eggs, 145

Coffin Pizza Pockets, 147

Moon Phase Fries, 149

Masque of the Red Death Skeleton Cookies, 151

Deviled Raven Eggs

Makes 12 deviled eggs

"Quoth the raven, 'Nevermore.'"
—"The Raven"

These clever little devils are dyed using a variation on the tea egg technique to create spidery black lines, and the striking green color of the filling comes from avocado.

INGREDIENTS

6 eggs
Black gel
   food coloring
1 medium avocado
1 teaspoon
   lemon juice
1 teaspoon fresh
   flat-leaf parsley,
   finely chopped
¼ teaspoon cumin
¼ teaspoon
   garlic powder
¼ teaspoon salt
¼ teaspoon pepper

INSTRUCTIONS

1 Place the eggs in the bottom of a large saucepan. Fill with cold water until the eggs are under approximately 2 inches of water. Place on high heat. When the water comes to a boil, remove from heat and cover for 7 minutes. Drain and allow the eggs to cool.

2 Fill 3 large mugs about ⅔ full with cold water. Place the mugs on a baking sheet to avoid staining anything if they spill. Put 3 to 4 drops gel food coloring in each mug and stir until completely dissolved.

3 When the eggs are cooled, gently crack each one in several places by tapping them against the counter and rotating as you tap. Try to create a lot of tiny cracks but not so many that the shell falls off.

4 Leaving the cracked shell in place, lower 2 eggs into each mug of food coloring. Put the mugs in the fridge for 7 to 12 hours.

5 Remove the eggs from the mugs and pat dry with a paper towel. Gently peel the shell from each egg, revealing the spiderweb pattern underneath. The color will be closer to a deep indigo than a true black.

6 Cut each egg in half lengthwise and set the yolk halves aside in a bowl. Set the white halves on a serving plate (or a 9" x 13" sealable container, if not serving right away).

7 Add the yolks to a medium bowl with all the remaining ingredients and mash until well combined. Transfer to a piping bag fitted with a large star tip (such as a Wilton 1M tip).

8 Pipe filling into each egg half. If not serving right away, cover tightly with plastic wrap and chill in the refrigerator until ready to serve.

Serve upon a midnight dreary!

Coffin Pizza Pockets

Makes 9 pizza pockets

"This coffin was warmly and softly padded, and was provided with a lid, fashioned upon the principle of the vault-door, with the addition of springs so contrived that the feeblest movement of the body would be sufficient to set it at liberty."
—"The Premature Burial"

The recipe described here makes margherita pizza pockets, but you can change up the fillings and use pepperoni, barbeque chicken, green pepper and sausage, or any of your other favorite pizza toppings.

INGREDIENTS

1 (13.8-oz.) can Pillsbury classic pizza dough
4½ tablespoons sun-dried tomato pesto (see page 245)
2.3 ounces fresh mozzarella
9 medium basil leaves
1 egg mixed with 1 tablespoon water, for egg wash
¼ teaspoon garlic powder
¼ teaspoon onion powder
¼ teaspoon salt

Special Tools

2" x 3½" coffin cookie cutter

INSTRUCTIONS

1 Preheat oven to 375°F. On a lightly floured surface, roll out pizza dough into a 10" x 14" rectangle. Use a coffin cookie cutter to cut out 18 coffins.

2 Transfer 9 coffins to an ungreased baking sheet, spacing them evenly apart. Spread ½ tablespoon pesto across each coffin, leaving a ¼-inch border. Top with basil leaves.

3 Cut mozzarella into ⅜-inch-wide slices. Cut slices into 9½" x 2" planks. Place 1 plank onto each basil leaf.

4 Brush edges of pizza dough with egg wash and place remaining coffin shapes on top. Crimp edges with a fork. Brush tops with remaining egg wash. Sprinkle with garlic powder, onion powder, and salt.

5 With a knife, cut short, thin strips of dough from the coffin scraps. Arrange on coffins in the shape of crosses.

6 Bake for 15 minutes until tops are golden and the tips of the crosses are just beginning to brown. Remove from the pan with an offset metal spatula and transfer to a wire rack to cool slightly for 5 to 10 minutes.

Serve warm while reading some spooky tales!

Moon Phase Fries

Makes approximately 28 fries and ½ cup ketchup

"Suddenly there shot along the path a wild light, and I turned to see whence a gleam so unusual could have issued. . . . The radiance was that of the full, setting, and blood-red moon, which now shone vividly through that once barely-discernible fissure."
—"The Fall of the House of Usher"

For optimal effect, look for potatoes that have a circular circumference, rather than oblong. This will ensure the fries look moonlike, rather than squat.

INGREDIENTS

For the Ketchup
½ cup ketchup
2 tablespoons sweet Thai chili sauce
3 teaspoons lime juice

For the Fries
3 red potatoes
1 tablespoon olive oil
1¾ teaspoons steak seasoning of choice
1 tablespoon fresh parsley, finely chopped

Special Tools

2½-inch round cookie cutter

INSTRUCTIONS

1 To make the ketchup, stir all ingredients together in a small bowl and set aside.

2 To make the fries, begin by preheating oven to 400°F. Thoroughly rinse and dry potatoes and cut into ¼-inch-thick slices, discarding the ends (each potato should make approximately 7 slices).

3 Leave the slices of the first potato whole (these will be full moons). Cut the slices from the second potato in half width-wise to make half-moons. Use a 2½-inch round cookie cutter to turn the slices from the remaining potato in gibbous and crescent shapes by cutting a curved line through each disk slightly left or right of center. This will create both the crescent and the gibbous. Note that there will be twice as many half-moons as other shapes. If desired, you can use only 4 slices to make half-moons and use the remaining slices from the same potato to make other shapes.

4 Add pieces to a medium bowl with olive oil and gently toss to combine.

5 Place full and gibbous moons on a greased baking sheet. Sprinkle both sides of each slice with steak seasoning and parsley. Bake for 10 minutes or until soft and easily punctured with a fork.

6 Repeat Step 5 with half-moons and crescent moons.

7 Transfer to a serving plate with ketchup mix.

Serve on a midnight dreary!

Masque of the Red Death Skeleton Cookies

Makes 12–18 cookies

"And Darkness and Decay and the Red Death held illimitable dominion over all."
—"The Masque of the Red Death"

Gingerbread men aren't just for Christmas! You can change up the flavors and icing decorations for all seasons. These sweet skeletons are red velvet cookies with cream cheese frosting.

INGREDIENTS

For the Cookies
1¼ cups flour
¾ cup unsweetened cocoa powder
½ teaspoon baking powder
¼ teaspoon salt
½ cup butter
2 tablespoons vegetable shortening
¾ cup sugar
1 egg
2 tablespoons milk
2 teaspoons vanilla extract
1½ teaspoons red gel food coloring

For the Frosting
¼ cup butter
4 ounces cream cheese, softened
1½ cups powdered sugar
¾ teaspoon vanilla extract

Special Tools

3½-inch gingerbread man cookie cutter

INSTRUCTIONS

1 To make the cookies, in a medium bowl, whisk together the dry ingredients and set aside.

2 In the bowl of a standing mixer, beat butter, shortening, and sugar on medium speed until combined. Beat in the egg, milk, vanilla, and food coloring, stopping to scrape the sides of the bowl if necessary.

3 Gradually beat in the flour mix on low speed. Gradually bring the speed up to high and beat until combined.

4 Separate dough into two equal balls and flatten into 4 inch disks. Wrap in plastic and chill in the refrigerator 1 to 2 hours or until firm but not hard. While waiting, preheat oven to 325°F.

5 Place the first disk between 2 sheets of wax paper and roll to just under ¼-inch thickness. Cut out 6 gingerbread men and transfer to an ungreased baking sheet.

6 Bake 13 minutes or until edges are firm and center is set. Remove from oven and allow to cool on the pan for 3 minutes. Using an offset metal spatula, remove to a wire rack to cool. Roll out, cut, and bake 6 more gingerbread men from remaining disk of dough. If desired, reroll scraps to cut out more gingerbread men.

7 To make the frosting, beat the butter and cream cheese together in a large bowl with a hand mixer at medium speed until combined. Sift in 1 cup powdered sugar until combined. Beat in vanilla until combined. Sift in remaining powdered sugar and beat until combined, adding additional powdered sugar if necessary to reach desired consistency.

8 Transfer frosting to a piping bag fitted with a medium round piping tip. Pipe skeleton bones onto cookies.

9 Chill in the refrigerator until 1 hour before serving.

Serve to the Red Death to convince it spare you!

Snacks for Sleuths

Sherlock Holmes

By Sir Arthur Conan Doyle

"Sherlock Holmes was, as I expected, lounging about his sitting-room in his dressing-gown . . . and smoking his before-breakfast pipe. . . . He received us in his quietly genial fashion, ordered fresh rashers and eggs, and joined us in a hearty meal."

—"The Adventure of the Engineer's Thumb"

Menu

Blood Orange Scones, 155

Roasted Tomato Deviled Scotch Eggs, 157

Sherlock's Steak Sandwiches, 161

London Fog Mystery Cookies, 163

Blood Orange Scones

Makes 8 scones

"Opening [the envelope] hurriedly, out there jumped five little dried orange pips, which pattered down upon his plate."
—"The Five Orange Pips"

This reinterpretation of the classic British scone is inspired by "The Five Orange Pips," one of Sherlock Holmes's most difficult cases. Luckily, this citrusy scone is delicious enough to make you forget even your peskiest case. The outside has a firm, sweet crust, and the inside is tender with a distinct orange flavor. This recipe uses blood orange bitters instead of juice, which means you can make it even if blood oranges aren't in season!*

INGREDIENTS

2 cups flour
¼ cup sugar, plus
⅜ teaspoon for dusting
2 teaspoons
baking powder
½ teaspoon baking soda
½ teaspoon salt
⅓ cup cold
butter, divided
into tablespoons
1 tablespoon orange zest
(or blood orange zest,
if they're in season)
1 egg, lightly beaten
¼ cup blood
orange bitters
¼ cup cold half-and-half
1 tablespoon milk, for
brushing on top

INSTRUCTIONS

1 Preheat oven to 425°F. Line a baking sheet with parchment paper and set aside.

2 Whisk the flour, ¼ cup sugar, baking powder, baking soda, and salt together in a large bowl. With a fork or pastry blender, cut the butter into the flour mix until the mix has a crumb-like texture with bits of pea-sized butter throughout. Stir in the zest and make a well in the center of the flour mix.

3 Add the beaten egg to the well. Mix the bitters and half-and-half together. Pour that into the well also. Stir it all up with a fork until just combined. The dough will be damp and a little sticky (don't work it too much, because that can make the scones tough).

4 Shape the dough into a ball with your hands, making sure to press any stray bits from the bottom of the bowl into the ball. Place it on the prepared baking sheet and flatten it into a 7½- to 8-inch round disk. Use a sharp knife to score the dough into triangles. Cut about halfway through the dough to ensure that the lines don't disappear while baking (cutting halfway through without completely separating allows the scones to retain more moisture than if they were baked as individual triangles, while still keeping the lines of the individual portions visible).

5 Brush the top of the dough with milk and sprinkle on the ¾ teaspoon sugar.

(Continued on next page)

6 Bake for 15 to 20 minutes or until the center is fully set and the top is golden brown. Don't worry if the top browns well before the center is finished. The crust sets a bit early, but it shouldn't burn. Instead, keep an eye on the center. If it looks wet and uncooked, leave it in the oven. Once the center has just begun to look fully set, take it out.

7 Allow to cool on the pan for 5 minutes. When ready to serve, slice along the lines you scored earlier.

Serve warm with Devonshire cream and jam while solving a tough case!

*Blood oranges are in season from December to May.

Roasted Tomato Deviled Scotch Eggs

Makes 12 deviled Scotch eggs

*"He was in his most cheerful and debonair humour. 'My dear Watson,
when I have exterminated that fourth egg I shall be ready to put you in touch
with the whole situation.'"*
—"The Valley of Fear"

These would also be delicious with bacon bits on top—making it almost a full English breakfast in one deviled egg!

INGREDIENTS

7 eggs, divided
**2¼ teaspoons salt,
   divided**
1½ cups cherry tomatoes
1 tablespoon olive oil
¾ cup panko crumbs
**12 ounces finely ground
   breakfast sausage**
**⅜ teaspoon pepper,
   divided**
**Approx. 6 cups
   vegetable oil**
2 tablespoons mayonnaise
**¼ teaspoon
   smoked paprika**
1 green onion

Special Tools

Candy thermometer

INSTRUCTIONS

1 Place 6 eggs and 1 teaspoon salt in the bottom of a medium-sized pot. Fill with cold water until the eggs are under approximately 2 inches of water. Place on high heat. When the water comes to a boil, remove from heat and cover for 6 minutes. Drain and allow the eggs to cool.

2 While the eggs cool, preheat oven to 375°F. In a medium bowl, combine tomatoes, olive oil, and ¼ teaspoon salt. Toss to combine. Spread tomatoes in an even layer on a baking sheet and place in oven for 25 minutes until tomatoes have split and several are beginning to brown on top. Remove from oven and transfer tomatoes to a blender. Blend until smooth and transfer to a large bowl (it should yield approximately 6 tablespoons of tomato mix). Set aside.

3 Lightly beat the remaining egg in a small bowl and set aside. Place the panko crumbs in another small bowl and set aside. If the sausage is in casings, remove the casings and discard. Place the sausage in a medium-sized bowl. Knead in ½ teaspoon salt and ¼ teaspoon pepper into the sausage.

4 Fill a medium-sized pot with vegetable oil approximately 2 inches deep and place over medium heat until oil reaches 350°F (if you flick in a bit of panko, it should sizzle energetically).

5 While the oil heats, wrap the eggs us thinly as possible in the sausage. Do this by dividing the sausage mix into

(Continued on page 159)

6 equal pieces and shaping these into balls. Flatten a ball in your palm and place an egg in the center. Press the sausage around the egg until it is completely encased with no gaps. Repeat for all the remaining eggs. Roll the sausage-wrapped eggs in the beaten egg. Then roll them in the panko crumbs.

6 Lower 2 to 3 eggs into the oil and cook for 3 minutes or until the breading is golden brown and the sausage is cooked through (cut into the sausage layer of 1 egg to check for doneness). Remove the eggs with a slotted spoon or tongs and set them on a plate lined with a paper towel for 5 minutes.

7 Repeat Step 6 with remaining eggs. Allow eggs to rest for 10 minutes or until room temperature.

8 Slice each egg in half lengthwise and gently scoop out the yolks, transferring them to the large bowl with the tomato mix. Add mayonnaise, smoked paprika, scant 1/2 teaspoon salt, and 1/8 teaspoon pepper. Blend with a hand mixer on medium speed until smooth.

9 Transfer egg filling to a piping bag fitted with a large round piping tip (such as a Wilton #2A). Pipe filling into eggs.

10 Cut green onion into small pieces and place 3 pieces on each egg.

Serve to your favorite British detective!

Sherlock's Steak Sandwiches

Makes 2 large sandwiches (can be cut into halves or quarters)

"He cut a slice of beef from the joint upon the sideboard, sandwiched it between two rounds of bread, and thrusting this rude meal into his pocket he started off upon his expedition."
—"The Adventure of the Beryl Coronet"

Sherlock Holmes is famous for having a sparse appetite, but cold beef sandwiches seem to be a weakness of his. He indulges in them several times throughout the books, mostly while traveling on a case. I can see why! What could be better brain food than hearty bread, protein that sticks to your ribs, and some choice toppings to wake your taste buds?

INGREDIENTS

For the Sauce
3 tablespoons sour cream
2 tablespoons horseradish sauce
1 strong pinch kosher salt
1 strong dash black pepper
¾ teaspoon lemon juice

For the Sandwiches
½ lb. boneless steak cut into 2 portions*
Salt and pepper, to taste
4 slices whole wheat bread
4 radishes
1½ cups arugula

INSTRUCTIONS

1 Mix all the sauce ingredients together in a small bowl. Set aside.

2 Season the steak with salt and pepper to taste. Lightly oil a skillet and set on medium heat. When the skillet is hot, sear the steak for 2 minutes on both sides. Hold the short ends down on the skillet with a pair of tongs for 10 seconds each, just long enough to seal in the juices. Set the steak aside on a plate to rest.

3 Toast the bread. Thinly slice the radishes to about ¼-inch thickness.

4 Spread sauce on a slice of bread and arrange some arugula on top (this will act as a moisture barrier against the meat). Place the slices from one radish on top. Slice the steak into ½-inch-wide strips and place half of them on top of the radish layer. Add another layer of radish and then more arugula. Spread sauce on another piece of bread and place it on top.

5 Repeat Step 4 for the second sandwich.

6 Cut the sandwiches into halves or quarters if desired.

Pack them to go as you run off to crack the case!

Note: The sandwiches pictured use boneless chuck eye steak.

London Fog Mystery Cookies

Makes 10 cookies

"It was a September evening, and not yet seven o'clock, but the day had been a dreary one, and a dense drizzly fog lay low upon the great city."
—"The Sign of the Four"

These cookies are just as much an activity as they are a dessert. Use as many kinds of candy as you want (just make sure they're small enough to fit inside the cookie). You can even write sleuth-y fortunes to hide inside, like "An estranged uncle will leave you a large inheritance" or "A glamorous stranger will ask you for help solving a crime."

INGREDIENTS

For the Cookies
2 cups flour
½ teaspoon
    baking powder
¼ teaspoon salt
½ cup plus 2 tablespoons
    butter, softened
¾ cup sugar
1 egg
2 tablespoons milk
2 teaspoons
    vanilla extract

For the Frosting
3 tablespoons milk
2 bags Earl Grey tea
3 cups powdered sugar
¾ cup butter, softened
1½ teaspoons
    vanilla extract
6 drops black gel
    food coloring

For the Mystery Contents
10 tablespoons small
    candies, various
    kinds (I recommend
    2 tablespoons each of
    5 different varieties.*)

Special Tools

3-inch round cookie cutter
2½-inch round cookie cutter

INSTRUCTIONS

1 To make the cookies, in a medium bowl, stir together the flour, baking powder, and salt. Set aside.

2 In the bowl of a standing mixer, beat the butter and sugar on medium-high speed until fluffy, stopping to scrape the sides of the bowl if necessary. Beat in the egg, milk, and vanilla.

3 Set the mixer to low speed and gradually beat in the flour mix. When it has all been added, gradually adjust the speed to high and beat until just combined, stopping to scrape the sides of the bowl if necessary.

4 Divide the dough into 2 balls and flatten into 4-inch disks. Wrap tightly in plastic wrap and chill in the refrigerator for 1 hour or until firm but not hard.

5 Preheat oven to 325°F. On a floured surface, roll out the first disk to ⅛-inch thickness and cut out 10 (3-inch) circles, placing them evenly apart on an ungreased baking sheet. Shape the scraps into another 4-inch disk. Rewrap the disk and place in the refrigerator.

6 Place the baking sheet in oven for 12 minutes or until cookie edges are just beginning to brown and centers are

(Continued on next page)

set. Gently transfer to a wire rack to cool using an offset spatula (do this immediately, since the cookies can begin to stick to the sheet as they cool).

7 Repeat Steps 5 and 6 with the second disk of dough.

8 Roll out the first set of scraps and cut out 10 more circles (rerolling the dough if necessary). Transfer to a baking sheet. Using a 2½-inch cutter, cut out the center from each circle so you are left with a hollow ring. Bake for 6 minutes. Gently transfer to a wire rack to cool using an offset spatula.

9 Repeat Step 8 with your second set of scraps. When you're finished, you should have 20 circle cookies and 20 ring cookies.

10 To make the frosting, add the milk to a small, sealable container. Cut the teabags open and pour in the tea (discard the bags). Stir together gently. Cover and place in the fridge to steep for 2 hours.

11 Sift the powdered sugar into a small bowl and set aside. Beat the butter on medium speed in a standing mixer until smooth. Beat in 1 cup of the powdered sugar until combined, stopping to scrape the sides of the bowl if necessary. Beat in the vanilla extract and 1 tablespoon of Earl Grey milk mix (including tea leaves). Alternate beating in the remaining powdered sugar and milk.

12 Transfer ½ cup (approximately ¼ of the full batch) to a small bowl and stir in 6 drops black gel food coloring. Set aside.

13 Transfer the remaining frosting to a piping bag fitted with a medium star tip (such as a Wilton #32 tip). Pipe a flat layer of frosting onto 10 of the circle cookies using a spiral motion.

14 Transfer the black frosting to a piping bag fitted with a medium round piping tip (such as a Wilton #12 tip) and pipe large question marks onto each of the decorated cookies.

15 To construct the cookies, take a blank circle cookie for the base. Pipe a dab of leftover frosting on each of the four compass points and gently press a ring cookie in place over the base, wiping away any icing that oozes out with a finger. Pipe four more dabs of icing on top of the ring and place another ring over it. This will create a pocket. Fill the pocket with 1 tablespoon of small candies. Apply more icing to the top of the second ring and place a decorated cookie over the top.

16 Repeat Step 15 with the remaining cookies.

Serve on a misty autumn day as you puzzle over clues in your London apartment!

*Mini M&Ms offer the most complementary flavor to the Earl Grey icing, but you can also use Reese's Pieces, Nerds, sprinkles, or even small cereals like Fruity Pebbles or Cocoa Krispies.

Raspberry Curd

* Keep chilled *

A Technicolor Banquet

The Wonderful Wizard of Oz

By L. Frank Baum

"Within a short time she was walking briskly toward the Emerald City,
her silver shoes tinkling merrily on the hard, yellow road-bed.
The sun shone bright and the birds sang sweetly."

Menu
Emerald City Popcorn, 169
Pizza Pinwheel Cyclones, 171
Melted Witch Chips and Guacamole, 173
Pumpkin Winged Monkey Bread, 175

Emerald City Popcorn

Makes 11 cups popcorn

"Dorothy and her friends were at first dazzled by the brilliancy of the wonderful City. The streets were lined with beautiful houses all built of green marble and studded everywhere with sparkling emeralds."

This popcorn mix inspired by the Emerald City features green-tinted popcorn kernels and wasabi peas to represent the green of Oz's magnificent city and yellow-tinted popcorn kernels to represent the yellow brick road that leads there.

INGREDIENTS

5 tablespoons coconut oil, divided
⅓ cup popcorn kernels
1½ teaspoons turmeric
½ teaspoon salt
¾ cup pea crisps, crushed
½ teaspoon matcha powder, optional (for added color)
1 cup wasabi peas

INSTRUCTIONS

1 Melt 3 tablespoons coconut oil in a small bowl in the microwave and set aside.

2 Add remaining coconut oil to a large saucepan with high sides and place over medium-high heat. Add 3 popcorn kernels and partially cover with lid. When all three kernels have popped, quickly pour in all the remaining kernels in a single layer. Remove from heat for 30 seconds. Partially re-cover and place over medium high heat, shaking gently until most of the kernels have popped and the popping sound has reduced to 1 pop every 5 seconds. Transfer immediately to a large bowl. Add reserved coconut oil and salt and toss until well combined.

3 Transfer 3 cups popcorn to a medium bowl and stir in turmeric.

4 Sprinkle crushed pea crisps into remaining popcorn and stir to combine. Stir in matcha powder. Return turmeric popcorn to the large bowl and add wasabi peas. Toss to combine.

Serve to the heroes who slayed the Wicked Witch!

1
The Cyclone

orothy lived in the midst of the
with Uncle Henry, who
rmer's wife.

Pizza Pinwheel Cyclones

Makes 10 pinwheels

"The great pressure of the wind on every side of the house raised it up higher and higher, until it was at the very top of the cyclone; and there it remained and was carried miles and miles away as easily as you could carry a feather."

This version features pepperoni, but you can substitute crumbled sausage, fresh basil, ham and pineapple, or many other pizza toppings—as long as the pieces are diced small enough that you can still easily roll and cut the pastry dough. Just be aware that the addition of extra colors may make the pinwheel design harder to see.

INGREDIENTS

For the Pizza Sauce
¼ cup water
3 tablespoons
   tomato paste
1 clove garlic, minced
½ tablespoon butter
½ tablespoon olive oil
1 teaspoon red
   wine vinegar
1 teaspoon sugar
¾ teaspoon oregano
½ teaspoon onion powder
½ teaspoon paprika
¼ teaspoon salt
⅛ teaspoon pepper

For the Pinwheels
1 sheet frozen puff
   pastry, thawed
½ cup diced
   pepperoni slices
¾ cup shredded
   mozzarella cheese
1 egg mixed with
   1 tablespoon water, for
   egg wash

INSTRUCTIONS

1 Preheat oven to 375°F. Grease a baking sheet and set aside.

2 To make the pizza sauce, combine all sauce ingredients in a small saucepan over medium-high heat. Bring to a boil, stirring continuously. Reduce heat to low and allow to simmer for 5 minutes, stirring occasionally. Remove from heat and set aside.

3 To make the pinwheels, roll the puff pastry into a 10-inch square on a lightly floured surface and apply pizza sauce, spreading evenly but leaving 1 inch of the pastry exposed on 1 side. Sprinkle on the diced pepperoni slices and cheese, maintaining the exposed edge.

4 Brush exposed edge with egg wash and roll pastry into a tight spiral toward the washed edge. Just before completing the spiral, brush egg wash on the side of the spiral about to touch the exposed edge. Finish rolling so that the two washed edges meet. Press to adhere.

5 Slice the rolled pastry into 10 disks about 1 inch thick and place on the greased baking sheet. If the disks get slightly squashed while cutting, gently press them back into a circle shape.

6 Bake for 15 to 20 minutes until pastry is puffed and golden. Transfer to a serving plate.

Serve to Dorothy when she lands in Oz!

Melted Witch Chips and Guacamole

Makes 50 chips and 1½ cups guacamole

"This made Dorothy so very angry that she picked up the bucket of water that stood near and dashed it over the Witch, wetting her from head to foot . . . the Witch began to shrink and fall away. 'See what you have done!' she screamed. 'In a minute I shall melt away.'"

Making your own festively shaped baked tortilla chips is an easy way to amp up any holiday food spread.

INGREDIENTS

For the Chips
2 (10-inch)
   spinach tortillas
2 (10-inch)
   tomato tortillas
2 tablespoons olive oil
½ tablespoon kosher salt

For the Guacamole
2 medium avocados
1 Roma tomato, seeded
   and diced
½ cup diced red onion
2 teaspoons snipped
   fresh cilantro
1 clove garlic, minced
2 teaspoons lemon juice
½ teaspoon
   ground cumin
¼ teaspoon kosher salt

Special Tools

2½-inch witch hat
   cookie cutter
4-inch broom
   cookie cutter

INSTRUCTIONS

1 Preheat oven to 350°F. Use the hat cookie cutters to cut out 20 hats from the spinach tortillas.

2 Lightly brush both sides of each hat with olive oil and sprinkle with salt. Place on 2 ungreased baking sheets and bake hats for 6 minutes, flipping and rotating the pans halfway through. Transfer to a wire rack to cool.

3 Use the broom cutter to cut out 30 brooms from the tomato tortillas. Repeat Step 2 (there will most likely be a little oil and salt left over). *Bake brooms for only 5 minutes.*

4 To make the guacamole, peel and seed avocados and place in a medium bowl. Add all remaining ingredients and coarsely mash.

5 Transfer chips and guacamole to serving plate and bowl.

Serve to Dorothy and her friends after they defeat the Wicked Witch!

Pumpkin Winged Monkey Bread

Makes 1 (10-inch) monkey bread

"The Scarecrow and the Tin Woodman were rather frightened at first, for they remembered how badly the Winged Monkeys had treated them before; but they saw that no harm was intended, so they rode through the air quite cheerfully."

This easy dessert feeds a crowd and does a great job scratching that itch for pumpkin-flavored food we all get in autumn. The secret is a double whammy of flavor: pumpkin pie spice mixed in with the sugar coating and pumpkin puree in the glaze!

INGREDIENTS

¾ cup granulated sugar

1½ tablespoons pumpkin pie spice

3 (16-oz.) cans buttermilk biscuits

½ cup butter

1 cup brown sugar, packed

6 tablespoons canned pumpkin puree

2 ounces cream cheese

1 cup powdered sugar

1 tablespoon milk

INSTRUCTIONS

1 Preheat oven to 350°F. Coat the inside of a 10-inch tube pan with cooking spray and set aside. In a large bowl, stir together the granulated sugar and pumpkin pie spice. Set aside.

2 Open 1 can of biscuits and separate the biscuits. Cut each one in half and roll into a ball. Roll each ball in the sugar mix until well-coated and place in the tube pan.

3 Repeat Step 2 for the remaining cans of biscuits.

4 Bake for 40 minutes or until the top is firm and deep golden brown. Allow to rest in the pan for 10 minutes.

5 While the bread rests, make the glaze by mixing the butter, brown sugar, and pumpkin puree together in a small saucepan on medium heat until smooth. Bring to a boil. Cook and stir for 1 minute. Remove from heat.

6 Loosen bread from pan and overturn onto a serving plate. Brush with glaze.

7 In a medium bowl, beat the cream cheese with a hand mixer on medium speed until fluffy. Sift in the powdered sugar and beat until combined. Beat in the milk until combined. Transfer mix to a piping bag fitted with a ¼-inch round tip and pipe over monkey bread. Cover and chill in the refrigerator until ready to serve.

Serve to the winged monkeys to celebrate their liberation from the Wicked Witch!

While most holidays focus on the here and now, New Year's Eve is unique in that it has one eye fixed on the future. As each year comes to a close, we can't help but notice areas of our lives that could use improvement, giving rise to the New Year's focus on personal growth.

Character growth is a vital part of storytelling. Most characters don't experience it as literally as, say, Alice from *Alice's Adventures in Wonderland*, but it's still a hallmark of compelling literature. Growth is what allows Erik to release Christine in *The Phantom of the Opera* and Gerda to rescue Kai in "The Snow Queen." Characters who shutter their hearts and reject growth—such as the Snow Queen herself—are often doomed to destruction.

However, it's important not to ignore the lessons of our past. A year already lived may not have the shiny spotlessness of a new one, but it has the patina of wisdom that only experience can provide.

So, this New Year's Eve, as you nibble Eat Me Cakes and sip Drink Me Punch, resolving that *next* year will be better, *next* year will be different—allow yourself a moment of congratulations. After all, as important as it is to open your heart to new experiences and shed the flaws of the past, it's just as important to remember that you've grown a great deal already.

A Mad New Year's Party

Alice's Adventures in Wonderland
By Lewis Carroll

"There was a table set out under a tree in front of the house, and the March Hare and the Hatter were having tea at it. . . . 'No room! No room!' they cried out when they saw Alice coming. 'There's plenty of room!' said Alice indignantly, and she sat down in a large arm-chair at one end of the table."

Menu
Card Suit Cheese Bites, 181
The Queen of Hearts's Tomato Tart, 183
Herbed Mushroom Puffs, 187
Eat Me Cakes, 189

Card Suit Cheese Bites

Makes 16 cheese bites

"First came ten soldiers carrying clubs . . . oblong and flat, with their hands and feet at the corners: next the ten courtiers; these were ornamented all over with diamonds. . .After these came the royal children; there were ten of them . . . they were all ornamented with hearts. Next came the guests, mostly Kings and Queens."

These cheesy, savory vegetable appetizers are easy to whip up for New Year's Eve, a mad tea party, or an unbirthday party.

INGREDIENTS

2 red peppers
  (6.6 oz. each)
1 (1.5-lb.) eggplant
1 tablespoon olive oil
½ teaspoon salt
¼ teaspoon pepper
1 (8-oz.) chunk
  feta cheese
1 (16-oz.) log fresh
  mozzarella cheese
8 sprigs fresh rosemary,
  1½ inches long
8 sprigs fresh thyme,
  1½ inches long

Special Tools

2" card suit cookie
  cutters (diamond,
  heart, spade, and club)

INSTRUCTIONS

1 Preheat oven to 375°F. Cut the top from one of the peppers and discard. Cut out the seeded portion from the middle and discard. Cut the pepper in half lengthwise and trim the sides so that each half lays mostly flat. Turn the halves skin-side down on a cutting board and use the cookie cutters to cut 4 diamonds from one pepper half and 4 hearts from the other. Transfer to a large bowl. Repeat with the remaining pepper.

2 Cut the top from the eggplant and discard. Cut the eggplant in half lengthwise. Scoop out and discard the seeded portion. Trim the sides so that each half lays mostly flat. Use the cookie cutters to cut out 8 spades and 8 clubs. Transfer those to the large bowl with the diamonds and hearts (there should be 32 shapes total).

3 Add oil, salt, and pepper to the bowl and stir gently until combined.

4 Place the shapes skin-side up in a single layer on a lightly greased baking sheet. Place in the oven for 15 minutes.

5 While you wait, rinse and dry the cookie cutters. Cut the chunk of feta in half and cut each half into ¼-inch-thick planks (cutting it in half first helps prevent crumbling as you slice the planks). Cut 4 spades and 4 clubs from the feta, using a toothpick to loosen the edges from the cutter to avoid crumbling if necessary. Cut the mozzarella into ¼-inch-thick slices and cut 4 diamonds and 4 hearts from it.

(Continued on next page)

6 Using an offset metal spatula, gently transfer the shapes to a cutting board.

7 Stack the cheese and vegetable pieces so that each piece of feta is between 2 pieces of eggplant and each piece of mozzarella is between 2 pieces of red pepper. Use a toothpick to skewer a hole through the middle of each stack.

8 Strip all but the top leaves from the sprigs of rosemary (the leaves will be visible when sticking out the top). Stick a sprig of rosemary in the hole of each eggplant stack and a sprig of thyme in the hole of each pepper stack.

Serve to the Red Queen's gardeners after a long day of painting roses!

Sometimes dull cookie cutters have trouble cutting through the skin of vegetables. To deal with this, you can place the vegetable on a cutting board, place the cookie cutter on top, and gently strike it with the flat side of a meat mallet. If using this technique, be sure to hit the cutter squarely, not at an angle, otherwise it can bend the cutter. As such, it's best to only use this technique with cutters that are no larger than the striking side of the mallet.

The leftover vegetable scraps can be seasoned with olive oil, salt, pepper, and the leftover rosemary, then roasted and served with the cheese scraps as a snack, a side dish, or warm winter salad components.

The Queen of Hearts's Tomato Tart

Makes 1 (14-inch) tart

"In the very middle of the court was a table, with a large dish of tarts upon it: they looked so good, that it made Alice quite hungry to look at them—'I wish they'd get the trial done,' she thought, 'and hand round the refreshments!'"

Real-life re-creations of the Queen of Hearts's tarts are almost always sweet, so I decided to make a savory version with tomato and cheese filling. I highly recommend splurging for the cherry tomatoes on the vine; they create a striking visual effect and are much sweeter than those that have been plucked from the vine before packaging.

INGREDIENTS

For the Crust
1½ cups flour
¾ teaspoon salt
15 medium fresh
   basil leaves
7 tablespoons cold
   butter, cut into cubes

For the Filling
12 ounces crumbled
   goat cheese
1 cup ricotta
1 egg
3 cloves garlic, minced
¼ cup snipped
   green onion
1 teaspoon salt
¼ teaspoon pepper
12 ounces cherry
   tomatoes on the vine
Olive oil

Special Tools
6" x 14" rectangular
   tart pan with
   removeable bottom

INSTRUCTIONS

1 To make the crust, stir the flour and salt together in a large bowl. Set aside.

2 Make a stack of the basil leaves and roll lengthwise into a tight tube. Cut width-wise into thin strips. Chop these strips into small pieces. Transfer basil to the bowl with the flour mix and stir until combined.

3 Work the butter through the flour mix with fingers or a fork until it is well distributed. The mixture should have a texture like bread crumbs with some pea-size pieces of butter throughout. Stir in 7 tablespoons ice water, 1 tablespoon at a time, with a fork until the mixture holds together when pressed with fingers but isn't soggy. Gather the dough into a ball. Flatten and shape into a 3½" x 5" rectangle. Wrap in plastic wrap and chill in the refrigerator for at least 1 hour or until firm but not hard.

4 Preheat oven to 375°F. On a floured surface, roll out the dough into an 8" x 18" rectangle. Transfer to a 6" x 14" tart pan and trim edges to fit. Set aside.

5 To make the filling, in a medium bowl, stir together the goat cheese, ricotta, egg, garlic, green onion, salt, and pepper. Spread the cheese mix in an even layer in the bottom of the tart tin.

6 Place tomatoes on top with vines still attached and lightly brush with olive oil, making sure to coat the vines as well.

(Continued on page 185)

7 Bake for 1 hour or until tomatoes turn slightly brown on top and some begin to wrinkle. Allow to cool for 15 minutes before removing from tin. Remove stems just before slicing to serve.

Serve to the Queen of Hearts . . . but watch out for any knaves!

Herbed Mushroom Puffs

Makes 6 mushroom puffs

"After a while she remembered that she still held the pieces of mushroom in her hands, and she set to work very carefully, nibbling first at one and then at the other, and growing sometimes taller and sometimes shorter, until she had succeeded in bringing herself down to her usual height."

Give humble fungi a bit of flair with this easy yet elegant mushroom puff dish seasoned with onion, garlic, and a bit of fresh basil.

INGREDIENTS

1 box frozen puff pastry shells, thawed (contains 6 shells)
1 egg white
7 medium-size white button mushroom caps
½ Vidalia onion
1 clove garlic
1 tablespoon olive oil
1 teaspoon fresh basil, cut into chiffonade*
5–6 tablespoons canned cream of mushroom soup, unprepared
½ teaspoon kosher salt
¼ teaspoon fresh black pepper
Extra sprigs basil, for garnish (optional)

INSTRUCTIONS

1 Preheat oven to 425°F. Line a baking sheet with parchment paper. Break the puff pastry shells into individual pieces and space them evenly apart on the parchment.

2 Whisk the egg white with 1 tablespoon of water in a small bowl. Brush the tops of the shells with the egg wash. Bake 15 to 18 minutes or until risen and golden brown on top.

3 While you wait, thinly slice the mushroom caps, peel and dice the onion, and mince the garlic. Heat olive oil in a small skillet on medium low heat. Stir in mushrooms, onion, and garlic and cook until the onion is translucent, stirring regularly. Stir in basil, soup, salt, and pepper. Remove from heat.

4 When the shells are done, allow them to cool for 5 minutes on the baking sheet, then use a sharp knife to cut out the centers, taking care not to cut all the way down to the bottom. The center round should pull out several layers from the center when removed without taking the bottom with it.

5 Scoop 2 to 3 heaping spoonfuls of filling into each shell. Top with sprigs of basil for garnish, if desired.

Serve to Alice during her next visit to Wonderland!

Chiffonade is just a fancy word for little ribbons. To do this, place the leaves on top of each other, roll into a tight tube, and thinly slice width-wise into strips.

Eat Me Cakes

Makes 12 cupcakes

"Soon her eye fell on a little glass box that was lying under the table: she opened it, and found in it a very small cake, on which the words 'EAT ME' were beautifully marked in currants."

Red velvet cupcakes filled with gold and white sprinkles and topped with two-toned red and white cream cheese frosting roses. If that doesn't say "EAT ME," I don't know what does.

INGREDIENTS

**For the Red
Velvet Cupcakes**
½ cup plus
   2 tablespoons flour
¼ cup plus 2 tablespoons
   cocoa powder
½ teaspoon
   baking powder
¼ teaspoon baking soda
¼ teaspoon salt
¼ cup butter, softened
¾ cup sugar
1 teaspoon vanilla extract
2 eggs,
   room temperature
2½ tablespoons
   sour cream
¾ teaspoon distilled
   white vinegar
2½ teaspoons red gel
   food coloring
½ cup buttermilk
3 tablespoons
   gold sprinkles
3 tablespoons
   white sprinkles

**For the Cream
Cheese Frosting**
4 ounces cream cheese,
   softened

3 cups powdered sugar, divided
1 teaspoon vanilla extract
1 tablespoon milk
Approx. 8–10 drops red gel food coloring

For the Buttercream Frosting
¼ cup butter, softened
1 cup powdered sugar, divided
1 tablespoon milk
7 drops black gel food coloring

For the Decorations
4 Milano cookies
4 Oreos
Gold edible color spray

Special Tools
Melon baller

INSTRUCTIONS

1 To make the red velvet cupcakes, begin by preheating an oven to 350°F. Fill a cupcake pan with liners and set aside. In a medium bowl, whisk together all the dry ingredients except the sugar. Set aside.

2 In a large bowl, cream the butter on medium speed with a hand mixer. Beat in the sugar and vanilla until combined. Beat in the eggs 1 at a time. Beat in the sour cream and vinegar. Beat in the red gel food coloring. Alternate beating in the dry mix and buttermilk.

(Continued on next page)

3 Evenly divide the batter between the cupcake liners and bake for 15 to 18 minutes or until they spring back when tapped with a finger. Transfer cupcakes to a wire rack to cool.

4 When cool, use a melon baller to scoop out 1/2 tablespoon of cake from the center of each cupcake. Mix gold and white sprinkles together and fill each cupcake with sprinkles.

5 To make the cream cheese frosting, beat cream cheese in a medium bowl with a hand mixer on medium speed until fluffy. Sift in 1 cup powdered sugar and beat until combined. Beat in vanilla and milk. Sift and beat in remaining powdered sugar.

6 In a piping bag fitted with a large star tip, add 1 large spoonful of frosting. Add 2 drops of red gel coloring. Scoop in 2 large spoonfuls of frosting and add 2 more drops of coloring. Continue alternating frosting and coloring until the bag is full. Squish the bag in 3 to 4 spots where you see coloring to distribute it more evenly (no more than that or the color may get grainy). Pipe roses by starting in the center of each cupcake and circling outward in a spiral motion.

7 To make the buttercream frosting, beat butter in a medium bowl with a hand mixer on medium speed until smooth. Sift in 1/2 cup powdered sugar and beat until combined. Beat in milk and black gel coloring. Sift and beat in remaining powdered sugar. Transfer to a piping bag fitted with a small round writing tip (such as a Wilton #2 tip). Set aside.

8 To prepare the decorations, place the Milano cookies on a large sheet of wax paper and coat with edible color spray. Allow to dry. Use the black frosting to pipe the words "Eat Me" on each cookie. Place each cookie on top of a cupcake.

9 Using a small, sharp knife, separate the Oreos so that each open cookie has filling on only one side (using a knife prevents the circle of filling from breaking). Spray the blank cookie wafers (the ones without filling) with edible color spray, taking care to coat the sides as well. Use the knife to gently transfer the circle of filling to the gold cookies.

10 Use the black frosting to pipe a clock face onto each circle of filling. To draw it in the style of the cupcakes from the photograph, pipe roman numerals at the 12, 3, 6, and 9 positions and a black dot in the middle. Place each clock on top of a cookie.

11 Cover and chill cupcakes in the refrigerator until 1 hour before serving.*

Serve to the citizens of Wonderland to ring in the new year!

*Cakes with cream cheese frosting must be chilled when storing. However, it tastes best at room temperature. If making ahead of time, be sure to allow 1 hour for cupcakes to rest at room temperature before serving.

Note: Prep work for this recipe can be divided across multiple days. The frosted cupcakes can be made up to 2 days in advance (store covered and chilled). The Milanos and Oreos can be decorated up to 1 day in advance. These can be covered and stored at room temperature, then placed on cupcakes the day of serving.

A New Year's Masquerade

The Phantom of the Opera

By Gaston Leroux

"The supper was almost gay . . . the attention of some of the guests was diverted by their discovery, at the end of the table, of that strange, wan and fantastic face, with the hollow eyes, which had already appeared in the foyer of the ballet and been greeted by little Jammes' exclamation. 'The Opera ghost!'"

Menu
Devils on Horseback: Bacon-Wrapped Date, 195
Apple Rose Tartlets, 197
Savory Strawberry Éclairs, 199
Chocolate Strawberry Opera Cake, 203

Devils on Horseback: Bacon-Wrapped Dates

Makes 18 bacon-wrapped dates

"I knew what he had made of a certain palace at Mazenderan. From being the most honest building conceivable, he soon turned it into a house of the very devil, where you could not utter a word but it was overheard or repeated by an echo."

"Devils on Horseback" is the alternative name for bacon-wrapped dates, common and beloved hors d'oeuvres. Delightfully elegant yet simple to make, these sweet and salty nibbles are sure to capture everyone's heart—phantoms included!

INGREDIENTS

- 1 (12-oz.) package whole Medjool dates with pits (approx. 18 dates)*
- 12 strips bacon (regular, not thick-cut)

INSTRUCTIONS

1 Preheat oven 350°F. Line a baking sheet with aluminum foil and set aside. Cut a slit down the side of each date and ease out the pit with the end of your knife (don't worry about ruining the date; this isn't a delicate procedure).

2 Slice the bacon strips width-wise into thirds. Wrap one piece around each date with the seam on top. Wrap another piece over the top of each date, with the seam on the bottom.

3 Place your bacon-wrapped dates in rows on the baking sheet and bake for 30 to 40 minutes or until the bacon is crisp. Allow to rest on top of the stove for 5 to 10 minutes to cool slightly.

Serve warm to the mysterious inhabitant of the catacombs under the Paris Opera House!

*We're using dates that contain pits for this recipe because they are larger than pre-pitted dates even after the pit has been manually removed.

Apple Rose Tartlets

Makes 12 tartlets

"Why, he leaves them on the little shelf in the box, of course. I find them with the program, which I always give him. Some evenings, I find flowers in the box, a rose that must have dropped from his lady's bodice . . . for he brings a lady with him sometimes."
—Madame Giry

Roses are known to be the Phantom's calling card, so you're sure to win him over with these savory Gouda and caramelized onion tartlets, topped with apple rosettes.

INGREDIENTS

2 batches pie dough (See Deeper 'n Ever Turnip 'n Tater 'n Beetroot Pie recipe on page 101)
½ Vidalia onion
1 tablespoon olive oil
½ teaspoon salt
¼ teaspoon sugar
2.5 ounces Gouda cheese
2–3 Gala or Fuji apples*
Lemon juice

Special Tools

Mandoline

INSTRUCTIONS

1 Preheat oven to 350°F. Roll the pie dough to ⅛-inch thickness on a floured surface and cut into 4½-inch circles.

2 Thoroughly coat a muffin pan with cooking spray and gently lower the circles into the muffin wells. Prick the bottoms twice with a fork. Bake for 10 minutes. Allow to rest until completely cool (do not remove them from the muffin pan).

3 While waiting for the shells to cool, cut the onion into thin disks. Heat the olive oil in a large skillet on medium-low heat. Add the onions, stirring them around until completely coated with oil. Cover and allow to cook for 15 to 20 minutes until soft and translucent, stirring occasionally.

4 Turn up the heat to medium-high and stir in the sugar and salt. Continue to cook and stir until the onions are golden brown. Remove from heat and set aside.

5 Cut the Gouda into 12 disks approximately ¼-inch thick and 2 inches wide. Use them to line the bottom of the tart shells. For an easier but less exact alternative, cut the Gouda into small chunks and evenly distribute it between the tart shells.

6 Place pieces of onion equivalent to 1 to 2 full rings on top of each gouda disk.

7 Cut the apples into quarters and cut out the portions with seeds. Slice the quarters thin using the second setting

(Continued on next page)

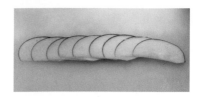

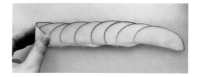

on a mandoline. As you cut, place the finished slices in a bowl and toss them with a few drops of lemon juice every so often to prevent browning.

8 Squirt some lemon juice on a cutting board and line up 10 apple slices overlapping each other in a straight line. Slowly roll the slices into a spiral, making sure to keep a good grip on the outside apples. For the most success with your apple roses, place each apple slice so that it lays halfway over the previous slice (this will provide structural stability). If the slices are thinner at one end, face the thin end toward the outside of the overlap (this will make rolling easier). Angle each slice just slightly downward, so that when you roll it up, the "petals" in the center will be higher, providing a more authentic rose look.**

9 Place the rolled rose in the center of one of the tart shells, pressing down to make sure it holds its shape. Repeat with all the remaining apple slices.

10 Bake for 10 to 15 minutes, until the apple slices are cooked through and the cheese has had time to melt. Keep a close watch on them for the last few minutes to make sure the edges of the petals don't start to burn.

11 Allow the tartlets to rest for 5 minutes in the pan, then ease them out with a butter knife onto a serving plate.

Serve a dozen or so of these delicious roses to the love of your life!

*You want the reddest apples you can find, since these will be sliced very thin to make rose petals. Bright red apples ensure clean red lines along the edges of the finished rosettes.

**If your apple slices are breaking as you roll them, you may be rolling too tightly. Try rolling the first few slices loosely, leaving a hole in the middle of your finished rose. Then tuck an extra slice or two in the middle after you place it in the tart.

Savory Strawberry Éclairs

Makes 26 (4-inch) éclairs

"Did the ghost really take a seat at the managers' supper-table that night, uninvited? And can we be sure that the figure was that of the Opera ghost himself? Who would venture to assert as much?"

This savory take on an elegant French confection balances the sweet-tart flavors of roasted strawberries and balsamic vinegar with the freshness of mint and whipped ricotta cheese.

INGREDIENTS

Choux Pastry
½ cup butter
1 cup water
1 cup flour
4 eggs

For the Filling
1 cup high-quality balsamic vinegar (from Modena)
1 lb. strawberries, quartered
¼ teaspoon salt
1½ cups ricotta
¾ cup pistachios, coarsely crushed
Mint leaves, for garnish

INSTRUCTIONS

1 To make the choux pastry, first move the oven racks to the top and bottom positions. Preheat oven to 400°F. Line 2 baking sheets with parchment paper or silicone mats and set aside.

2 Melt the butter and water together in a medium saucepan on low heat. Turn the heat to medium and bring to a boil. Turn off the heat and pour in the flour all at once. Stir together quickly with a silicone spatula. Turn heat back to medium. Cook for 2 minutes, stirring constantly. Remove from heat and transfer to a large mixing bowl. Beat in the eggs 1 tablespoon at a time with a hand mixer on medium speed until smooth.

3 Fit a piping bag with a ½-inch round piping tip and fill the bag with the pastry dough.

4 Pipe 13 (4-inch) éclairs at least 1½ inches apart on each baking sheet. Place the sheets in the oven. Bake for 20 minutes. Turn the heat down to 350°F; flip and rotate the pans. Bake for 20 minutes more. Turn off the heat and let the pastry shells sit for 10 minutes in the oven. Remove to a wire rack to cool.

5 Prepare the filling. To make the balsamic vinegar reduction, pour balsamic vinegar into a small sauté pan over medium heat and bring to a boil. Turn the heat to medium-low and allow to simmer for 15 minutes until slightly thickened. Remove from heat and allow to come to room temperature in the pan, approximately 15 minutes (makes 6 to 8 tablespoons).

(Continued on page 201)

6 To roast the strawberries, begin by preheating the oven to 400°F. Toss strawberries in salt. Spread them out on a lightly greased baking sheet and place in oven for 20 minutes, stirring halfway through. The strawberries should be soft and slightly darkened. Transfer to a blender and blend until smooth. Set aside.

7 Cut pastry shells in half lengthwise and set aside. Whisk ricotta for 1 minute or until fluffy. Transfer ricotta to a piping bag fitted with a large round tip (such as a Wilton 2A tip). Pipe approximately 1½ teaspoons of ricotta across the bottom half of each éclair. Sprinkle 1 teaspoon of pistachios onto each ricotta stripe.

8 Spoon approximately 1 teaspoon blended strawberries onto each éclair. Place the tops on the éclairs, pressing gently to adhere.

9 Drizzle balsamic vinegar reduction over the éclairs (approximately ¼ teaspoon per éclair). Place small mint leaves on top.

Serve at a masquerade ball!

Chocolate Strawberry Opera Cake

Makes 1 3¼" x 9" cake

"One day, tired of waiting for an opportunity, I moved the stone and at once heard an astounding music: the monster was working at his Don Juan Triumphant, with every door in his house wide open. I knew that this was the work of his life. I was careful not to stir."

Don't let this decadent dessert intimidate you: it's actually very easy! The recipe for each component is straightforward and fairly forgiving. The key to impressive presentation is perfectly even layers, so be sure to spread the fillings right up to the edge and check that each side of the cake is level before moving on to the next layer.

INGREDIENTS

For the Joconde
2 tablespoons butter
¾ cup almond flour
¾ cup powdered sugar
2 tablespoons all-purpose flour
3 eggs, lightly beaten
4 egg whites
1½ tablespoons granulated sugar

For the Buttercream
¾ cup butter, softened
3 cups powdered sugar, divided
1½ teaspoons almond extract
3 tablespoons milk, divided

For the Ganache
½ cup plus 2 tablespoons whipping cream, divided
2 cups semisweet chocolate chips

For the Strawberry Syrup
See recipe on page 248

For Garnish
9 small strawberries, leaves removed

INSTRUCTIONS

1 To make the joconde, begin by preheating an oven to 425°F. Line a 10" x 15" baking sheet with parchment paper or a silicone mat and set aside. Melt the butter in a small microwave-safe bowl and set aside.

2 In a medium bowl, sift together the almond flour, powdered sugar, and all-purpose flour. Whisk in the beaten eggs with a fork until combined. Set aside.

3 In the bowl of a standing mixer fitted with a whisk attachment beat the egg whites on medium speed until soft peaks form, approximately 2 minutes. With the mixer running, beat in the granulated sugar. Increase the mixer to full speed and continue to beat until the mixture makes stiff peaks, approximately 3 minutes.

4 Gently fold half the almond flour batter into the egg-white mix with a spatula. Fold in the remaining batter. Fold in the melted butter.

5 Pour the batter onto the prepared baking sheet. Spread out the batter with a large icing knife, taking care to make sure it is spread evenly throughout.

(Continued on next page)

6 Bake until the mixture springs back when lightly tapped with a finger, approximately 8 minutes. Remove from oven and flip joconde onto a silicone mat placed on a wire rack. Remove the parchment or silicone mat from the bottom and allow to cool.

7 To make the buttercream, use a hand mixer to beat the butter in a large bowl on medium speed until smooth. Sift in 1 cup powdered sugar and beat until fluffy. Beat in almond extract and 1 tablespoon milk. Alternate beating in remaining powdered sugar and milk until fully combined. Set aside.

8 To make the ganache, fill a small saucepan half full with water and bring to a boil over medium-high heat. Heat $1/2$ cup whipping cream in another small saucepan on low heat just until steaming, then remove from heat. Add the chocolate to a heat-safe bowl and place it on top of the pan with the boiling water. Turn off heat. Pour the steaming cream over the chocolate and allow to sit for 3 minutes. Whisk until smooth and set aside. Save the pan with the hot water for later.

9 Cut the joconde width-wise into 4 ($3^{1/2}$-inch-wide) pieces, trimming excess from the last piece if necessary.

10 To construct the cake, place 1 joconde piece spongy-side up on a wire rack placed over a baking sheet. Using a pastry brush, brush the layer with 3 tablespoons strawberry syrup. Add $1/3$ cup buttercream on top and spread until very even.*

11 Add another layer of cake and syrup. Spoon 5 tablespoons ganache on top and spread until even.

12 Add another layer of cake, syrup, and buttercream. Place the last cake layer on top and add the last layer of syrup. Set aside.

13 Bring the saucepan of water back to a boil and remove from heat. Place the bowl with the ganache on top and add 2 tablespoons cream. Whisk until combined. This will thin the ganache into a chocolate glaze.

14 Pour the glaze over the top of the cake and use a frosting knife to spread it into an even layer.

15 Chill uncovered in the refrigerator for 45 minutes until glaze is set. Evenly divide remaining buttercream between 2 piping bags, one fitted with a medium star piping tip and another with a writing tip.

16 Trim the sides from the cake to reveal the layers within. Cut into 9 (1-inch-wide) slices, wiping knife blade clean between slices.

17 Pipe a dollop of frosting onto one end of each slice using the star tip piping bag. Garnish with strawberries on top. Use the bag with the writing tip to pipe a treble clef on the other end of each slice.

Serve to the Phantom to congratulate him for finishing his opera!

*If desired, you can trim a piece of wax paper to the size of your cake layers, with a 1-inch lip on one side. When placed under the first layer of cake before constructing, this can make it easier to slide the cake from the rack when cutting.

Note: This recipe has quite a few components, so I recommend working ahead. The syrup and buttercream can be made and stored (the syrup in the fridge and the buttercream at room temp) up to 3 days early. The joconde can be made up to 2 days early. To store the joconde, you can keep it on the silicone mat and wrap it tightly with plastic wrap.

Winter Wonderland Dainties

"The Snow Queen"

By Hans Christian Andersen

"Many a winter's night she flies through the streets of the town, and peeps in at the windows; and they then freeze in so wondrous a manner that they look like flowers."

Menu
Fried Snowballs, 209
Savory Snowflake Bread, 211
Gerda's Cherry Bites, 215
Mirror Shard Mini Ice Cream Cakes, 217

Fried Snowballs

Makes 20 snowballs

"The snow-flakes grew larger and larger, till at last they looked just like great white fowls. Suddenly they flew on one side; the large sledge stopped, and the person who drove rose up. . . . It was the Snow Queen."

These delicious "snowballs" take the idea of a loaded potato and turn it into finger food! Coating them in panko crumbs instead of traditional bread crumbs offers a crisp crunch.

IINGREDIENTS

4 Yukon Gold potatoes
1 teaspoon salt, divided
2 eggs, divided
1 cup panko crumbs
½ cup sharp
   cheddar cheese
¼ cup green onions,
   chopped
3 tablespoons bacon bits
¼ teaspoon black pepper
6 cups vegetable oil (or
   enough to fill the pot
   2 inches deep)

INSTRUCTIONS

1 Peel and cut the potatoes into quarters. Add them to a medium-size pot and fill with cold water until potatoes are under 1 inch of water. Sprinkle in ½ teaspoon salt. Bring to a boil over medium-high heat. Continue to boil for 10 minutes or until fork-tender. Remove from heat and drain.

2 Transfer the potatoes to a large mixing bowl. Mash thoroughly and allow to cool for 20 minutes or until room temperature, stirring occasionally to release trapped heat.

3 Crack 1 egg into a small bowl and whisk with a fork; set aside. Pour the panko crumbs into another bowl and set aside as well.

4 When the potatoes are cool, add the second egg, cheese, green onions, bacon bits, pepper, and remaining salt to the mixing bowl. Stir until thoroughly combined.

5 Roll the potato mix into 1½-inch balls.

6 Pour the vegetable oil into a medium-sized saucepan and set the burner on medium-low heat. How long the oil will take to come to temperature will depend on the pan's materials and dimensions (lower heat takes longer to come to temperature but is easier to control). Ideal frying temperature is 350 to 375°F. For this recipe, I find the low end of that range to be preferable. If you do not have a cooking thermometer, you can test the oil by flicking a few panko bits into it. If they sizzle quickly but not aggressively, it should be ready.

(Continued on next page)

7 When the oil is almost ready, roll each ball first in the whisked egg, then in the panko crumbs. Lower 3 balls at a time into the oil and let them cook 2 to 3 minutes or until golden brown and heated through. You can cut one from the first batch in half to check how much time they'll need (the most important thing is to make sure the egg is fully cooked). With a slotted spoon or set of tongs, remove the balls from the oil and place them on a plate lined with a paper towel to drain. Keep in mind that you may need to wait a few minutes to allow the oil to come back up to temperature.

Serve warm after a lively snowball fight!

Savory Snowflake Bread

Makes 1 (12-inch) snowflake bread

"The flake of snow grew larger and larger; and at last it was like a young lady, dressed in the finest white gauze, made of a million little flakes like stars. She was so beautiful and delicate, but she was of ice, of dazzling, sparkling ice . . ."

This recipe's striking design comes from twisting the "branches" of the snowflake to reveal the sumptuous filling inside.

INGREDIENTS

3 sweet onions
1 tablespoon olive oil
3 tablespoons butter
1 teaspoon salt
4 (8-oz.) containers Pillsbury crescent dough
12 ounces fig jam
3 ounces grated Gruyère cheese
1 egg whisked with 1 tablespoon water, for egg wash

INSTRUCTIONS

1 Preheat oven to 350°F. Coat an 11½" x 17" baking sheet with cooking spray and set aside.

2 Peel onions and cut in half. Cut the halves into thin strips and set aside. Place olive oil and butter in a large sauté pan with tall sides over medium-low heat until butter is melted. Add onions and stir until well-coated. Cook for 30 minutes, stirring regularly, until translucent and soft. Stir in the salt and cook for another 35 to 45 minutes until very soft (almost jammy) and golden brown, stirring very regularly and keeping a close eye on the pot to avoid burning. Remove from heat and set aside.

3 Flour a large cutting board and unroll 1 can of crescent dough. Pinch the perforated lines of the dough closed on both sides. Flour the top of the dough and roll into an 11" x 12" rectangle. Cut out a 10-inch circle. Gingerly fold the circle in half and transfer to the baking sheet. Unfold circle and spread 3 ounces fig jam, ⅓ of the caramelized onions, and 1 ounce Gruyère over the circle in layers, making sure to coat the dough right up to the edge.

4 Repeat Step 3 twice, creating a total of 3 layers of dough, fig jam, onions, and cheese. Roll and cut the final can of dough into a circle and place on top. Starting 1 inch from the center of the circle, cut dough into 10 equal portions.

5 Grasp the ends of 2 adjoining portions and carefully twist each one twice, rotating away from each other.

(Continued on page 213)

6 Repeat Step 5 with remaining portions. Brush the top of the bread with egg wash and bake for 30 minutes or until golden brown on top. Run a long knife underneath the bread while warm to separate it from the pan. Allow to rest on the pan for 10 minutes, then transfer to a serving plate.

Serve at the court of the imposing Snow Queen!

Gerda's Cherry Bites

"On the table stood the most exquisite cherries, and Gerda ate as many as she chose, for she had permission to do so. While she was eating, the old woman combed her hair."

Cherries feature prominently throughout "The Snow Queen," so I whipped up these tiny tarts with a creamy, melted Camembert center and sweet-tart cherry preserves on top. Add a bit of fresh basil for an herbaceous note, and you've got an elegant, easy appetizer for a crowd ready in minutes!

INGREDIENTS

**3 ounces
  Camembert cheese
30 mini phyllo tart shells
½–¾ cup
  cherry preserves
2–3 large basil leaves**

INSTRUCTIONS

1 Preheat oven to 325°F. Cut Camembert into 30 pieces, each approximately ¼ inch wide and 1 inch long. Set aside.

2 On an ungreased baking sheet, evenly space 15 phyllo shells. Place 1 piece of cheese in each shell and top with 1 teaspoon cherry preserves. Bake for 15 minutes.

3 Repeat Step 2 with the remaining shells, cheese, and preserves.

4 Stack your basil leaves. Starting at the base of the leaves, roll them tightly into a tube. Cut the tube width-wise into thin strips. Sprinkle basil leaf strips over the tarts.

5 Allow to cool on the pan for at least 10 minutes before serving.

Serve warm to melt the shards of ice in the heart of a friend!

Mirror Shard Mini Ice Cream Cakes

Makes 10 ice cream "cupcakes"

"Higher and higher still they flew, nearer and nearer to the stars, when suddenly the mirror shook so terribly with grinning, that it flew out of their hands and fell to the earth, where it was dashed in a hundred million and more pieces."

This tasty reference to the fateful mirror from "The Snow Queen" features a no-bake shortbread crust, amaretto vanilla ice cream filling, and candy mirror pieces. A frosty treat sure to melt any frozen heart!

INGREDIENTS

- 1 cup shortbread cookie crumbs
- 2½ tablespoons crushed almonds
- 2 tablespoons unsalted butter, melted
- 2½ cups vanilla bean ice cream
- 2½ tablespoons amaretto
- 10 Jolly Ranchers, blue
- 8 ounces frozen whipped topping, thawed

INSTRUCTIONS

1 Fill a cupcake pan with cupcake liners and set aside. In a medium bowl, whisk together cookie crumbs, crushed almonds, and melted butter with a fork until well combined.

2 Spoon 2 tablespoons cookie crumb mix into each liner and firmly press flat. Freeze for 30 minutes.

3 In a medium bowl, beat together ice cream and amaretto with a hand mixer on medium speed until smooth. Divide ice cream evenly between cupcake liners (approximately ¼ cup per liner). Freeze for 1 hour.

4 Preheat oven to 350°F. Line a baking sheet with parchment paper and space Jolly Ranchers ½ inch apart on the parchment paper. Place in oven for 7 minutes or until melted. Remove and allow to cool. Using the end of a spoon, strike melted candy at intervals at least 3 inches apart (this will prevent the candy from breaking into pieces that are too small).

5 Fit a piping bag with a large star tip (such as a Wilton #1M tip) and fill with whipped topping. Pipe whipped topping onto frozen cakes. Place 3 candy shards on top of each cake. Freeze until ready to serve.

Serve to the Snow Queen to melt her frozen heart!

Festive Sips

Every holiday meal needs a festive drink to match. That's where these recipes come in! Curl up with a mug of Jo March's hot cocoa, whip up a batch of Nevermore cocktails at your next Halloween party, or ring in the new year with a glass of sparkling Drink Me Punch. The best part? They're all easy to make for a crowd!

Drink Me Punch

from Alice's Adventures in Wonderland, *by Lewis Carroll*

Makes 9 cups punch

"This time she found a little bottle on it . . . and tied 'round the neck of the bottle was a paper label, with the words 'DRINK ME' beautifully printed on it in large letters."

When hosting a New Year's Eve party, the last thing anyone wants is to be stuck mixing drinks all night. Stir up this big-batch punch recipe just before the party starts, and you're ready to go!

INGREDIENTS

3 cups lemonade, chilled
3 cups pomegranate
  juice, chilled
3 cups lemon-lime soda
  or Riesling, chilled
Lemon slices, for garnish

INSTRUCTIONS

1 Combine all ingredients except for the garnish in a large punch bowl or pitcher and stir to combine. Divide between glasses of desired size. Cut one slit in each lemon slice from the outer edge to the center and perch on the lip of the punch glasses.

Serve at a very merry unbirthday . . . or a New Year's Eve party!

Jo March's Hot Cocoa Mix

from Little Women, *by Louisa May Alcott*

Makes 4³/₄ cups powder (19 cups prepared cocoa)

*"'Thou shouldst save some for the little friend: sweets to the sweet, mannling,'
and Mr. Bhaer offered Jo some, with a look that made her wonder if chocolate
was not the nectar drunk by the gods."*

Prepare this to serve at a festive gathering or scoop the powder mix into mason jars to give as gifts! This hot cocoa pairs beautifully with the homemade marshmallows in this book, especially the gingerbread version, on page 239.

INGREDIENTS

2 cups powdered milk
1¾ cups powdered sugar
1 cup cocoa powder
Gingerbread
  marshmallows (see
  page 239)

INSTRUCTIONS

1 Thoroughly whisk all ingredients in a medium bowl and transfer to an airtight container.

2 To prepare, transfer ¼ cup cocoa mix to a mug and heat 1 cup milk in a small saucepan* on medium-low heat just until steaming, swirling the pan regularly. Pour hot milk into mug and stir thoroughly.

Serve to the March sisters!

*If you would rather avoid having a pot to wash, you can heat the milk in a mug for 1 to 2 minutes on high in a microwave, stirring the milk halfway through to prevent a skin from forming (be sure to use a microwave-safe mug). When the milk is steaming, stir in your cocoa mix.

The Phantom's Rose

from The Phantom of the Opera by Gaston Leroux

Makes 1 cocktail

"They were marvelous red roses that had blossomed in the morning, in the snow, giving a glimpse of life among the dead."

This cocktail's distinctive charred orange slice garnish plays two roles. Of course, it's visually striking, but it also adds a contrasting smoky flavor to the otherwise sweet, citrusy notes of the drink.

INGREDIENTS

3 ounces Rosa Regale red wine, chilled

1½ ounces triple sec, chilled

1 ounce blood orange bitters

1 round orange slice*

Special Tools

Chef's torch

INSTRUCTIONS

1 Combine wine, triple sec, and bitters together in a wineglass. Set aside.

2 On a clean, nonflammable surface (such as a granite countertop), use a chef's torch to scorch the top of the orange slice. Be sure to use the torch safely and in accordance with product guidelines. Lay the orange slice on top of the liquid in the glass, scorched-side up.

Serve to a prima donna after a performance at the Paris Opera House!

*Be sure the diameter of the orange slice is small enough to fit inside the glass. This may necessitate using a small orange or cutting from the narrow end of a larger orange instead of the middle.

Poe's Nevermore Cocktail

from "The Raven" by Edgar Allan Poe

Makes 1 cocktail

"Quoth the Raven 'Nevermore.'"

This refreshing, darkly sweet (but not too sweet) cocktail is just right for sipping at a Halloween party or a midnight poetry reading.

INGREDIENTS

¼ cup blueberries
2 large basil leaves
½ cup ice
3 ounces sweet
   blueberry wine
2 ounces black
   cherry juice
4 shakes
   Angostura bitters

INSTRUCTIONS

1 In the bottom of a cocktail shaker, muddle blueberries and basil leaves.

2 Add ice. Pour in wine, cherry juice, and bitters. Close shaker and shake vigorously to combine.

3 Pour into a wineglass and garnish with extra blueberries and basil if desired.

Serve upon a midnight dreary!

Pumpkin Cider

from "The Legend of Sleepy Hollow" by Washington Irving

Makes 6 cups cider

"On all sides he beheld vast store of apples; some hanging in oppressive opulence on the trees; some gathered into baskets and barrels for the market; others heaped up in rich piles for the cider-press."

This Thanksgiving try a twist on classic apple cider by flavoring it with homemade pumpkin syrup! This no-fuss recipe can be prepared in a slow cooker, then placed back in the same crock to keep warm while serving. You can even bottle any extra syrup to give as gifts so folks can flavor their own drinks at home.

INGREDIENTS

6 Fuji apples
2 Granny Smith apples
1 orange
2 cinnamon sticks
2 star anise seed pods
1 cup pumpkin syrup, plus more to taste (see recipe on page 247)

Special Tools

Slow cooker

INSTRUCTIONS

1 Core apples and cut into eighths. Peel orange and cut into quarters. Add to a slow cooker with cinnamon and anise. Pour 4 cups water over fruit mix.

2 Cover and heat on high for 5 hours. Pour mix through a colander into a large bowl. Discard fruit. Stir in pumpkin syrup until dissolved. Taste and add more if desired. To store, cover and chill in the refrigerator until 30 minutes before serving. To serve, pour liquid back into slow cooker and set heat to low.

Serve to guests to keep them warm on a brisk autumn evening!

The White Witch's White Chocolate Chai Latte

from The Lion, the Witch, and the Wardrobe, *by C. S. Lewis*

Makes 4 cups

"Edmund felt much better as he began to sip the hot drink. It was something he had never tasted before, very sweet and foamy and creamy, and it warmed him right down to his toes."

In *The Lion, the Witch, and the Wardrobe*, C. S. Lewis never says exactly what beverage the White Witch serves Edmund on his first trip to Narnia. We only know that it is "sweet and foamy and creamy" and wonderfully warm—a perfect description of a chai latte! This recipe includes a bit of melted white chocolate to make this drink truly special.

INGREDIENTS

6 chai tea bags
½ cup milk
¼ cup honey
3 tablespoons white
  chocolate chips

INSTRUCTIONS

1 Brew the tea bags for 7 minutes in 4 cups very hot water from a tea kettle. While you wait, heat the milk in a microwave-safe bowl or mug for approximately 30 seconds until hot and steaming.

2 Whisk honey and white chocolate chips into milk until chips are dissolved.

3 When tea is finished steeping, discard tea bags and transfer tea to a blender. Gradually add half the milk mix and blend for 1 minute. Add the remaining milk mix and blend for 1 minute more.

Serve warm to the Sons of Adam and Daughters of Eve!

Wicked Witch Punch

from The Wonderful Wizard of Oz, *by L. Frank Baum*

Makes 10 cups

"Well, in a few minutes I shall be all melted, and you will have the castle to yourself. I have been wicked in my day, but I never thought a little girl like you would ever be able to melt me and end my wicked deeds."

This sweet-tart punch has a fun bit of kick. Easy to make and easier to drink, it's just the thing to fill your glass when you toast the destruction of the Wicked Witch of the West.

INGREDIENTS

8 small kiwi fruit
1 cup lemon juice
   (squeezed from
   approximately
   8 lemons)
8 cups ginger ale, chilled
1¼ cups sugar

Special Tools

Wire-mesh strainer

INSTRUCTIONS

1 Peel and slice kiwi fruit into disks, discarding skins. Place in a blender and blend until liquified. Pour and press through a wire-mesh strainer into a bowl.

2 Combine all ingredients in a large pitcher and stir until sugar is dissolved.

Serve to celebrate the end of the Wicked Witch!

Delectable Gifts to Suit the Season

I may be biased, but I firmly believe that food makes the best gifts. As a consumable, it's a clever option for family and friends who want to avoid "more stuff." Additionally, food gifts are almost always more cost effective than store-bought options. You can even pair recipes to create a larger gift, such as a tasting set of infused sugars and honeys, cocoa mix with homemade marshmallows, or bread with flavored butter. Though especially fitting for Christmas, the food gifts you'll see here are versatile enough for any time of year.

Candied Walnuts

Makes 1 cup candied walnuts

Looking for a sweet but healthy gift to give? Sugar doesn't even make an appearance in this recipe! Instead, all the sweetness comes from a kiss of honey. This dessert's cozy flavors and homey feel make it a perfect gift.

INGREDIENTS

1 cup chopped walnuts
3 tablespoons honey
½ teaspoon apple
  pie spice
¼ teaspoon salt
¼ teaspoon
  vanilla extract

INSTRUCTIONS

1 Preheat the oven to 325°F. Line a baking sheet with tinfoil and coat the foil with cooking spray. Set aside.

2 Add all the ingredients to a medium bowl and stir until well combined. Spread the mix onto the tinfoil in a thin layer, breaking up the clumps as much as possible.

3 Bake for 10 minutes, stirring once halfway through.

4 Allow the nuts to cool on the pan (approximately 15 minutes). The coating on the nuts will harden.

5 When the nuts are completely cool, gently remove them from the foil and break the chunks into bite-size pieces.

Spiced Pine Nuts

Makes ½ cup nuts

These savory nuts are a match made in heaven with our Leek and Potato Soup with Parsnip and Garlic on page 99 and Smashed Pumpkin Soup on page 113, or seal them up in little mason jars with a bit of ribbon for guests to take home.

INGREDIENTS

½ cup pine nuts
1 teaspoon olive oil*
¼ teaspoon
  garlic powder
¼ teaspoon
  ground rosemary
¼ teaspoon onion powder
¼ teaspoon salt

INSTRUCTIONS

1 Preheat oven to 325°F. Add nuts and oil to a bowl and stir until well combined. Sprinkle in spices and stir.

2 Spread nuts out evenly on a baking sheet and toast 5 to 7 minutes until lightly browned, stirring nuts and rotating the pan halfway through. Allow to cool on the pan.

*Make sure to use 1 teaspoon of olive oil, not 1 tablespoon!

Flavored Butter

Makes ½ cup (8 tablespoons) flavored butter

If you like, you can make the butter itself from scratch using the recipe on page 87. Just note that it makes ½ cup plus 2 tablespoons of butter, rather than the ½ cup called for below, so adjust seasonings accordingly if using that recipe to make flavored butter.

INGREDIENTS

½ cup salted butter, softened

*If you would rather not gift the butter in a bowl, you can chill it until firm, shape it into a log (making sure your hands are very clean), and place it on a sheet of wax paper. Roll the log up in the paper and twist the open ends to close. For a decorative touch, tie bows around the twisted ends with kitchen twine or ribbon and apply a sticker label to the center of the wax paper featuring the name of the flavor.

INSTRUCTIONS

1 **For Honey Butter:** In a bowl, stir together butter and 1 tablespoon honey until smooth. If not using within 24 hours, cover and chill in the refrigerator until ready to use.

2 **For Lemon Dill Butter:** In a bowl, stir together butter, 1 tablespoon lemon juice, and 2 tablespoons finely chopped fresh dill. Cover with plastic wrap and allow to infuse at room temperature for 3 hours or in a refrigerator overnight. If not using within 24 hours, chill in the refrigerator until ready to use.

3 **For Garlic Herb Butter:** In a bowl, stir together butter, 2 cloves minced garlic, 1 teaspoon minced fresh rosemary, and 1 teaspoon fresh thyme. Cover with plastic wrap and allow to infuse at room temperature for 3 hours or in a refrigerator overnight. If not using within 24 hours, chill in the refrigerator until ready to use.

4 **For Parmesan Chive Butter:** In a bowl, stir together butter, 2½ tablespoons Parmesan cheese, and 2 tablespoons snipped fresh chives. Cover with plastic wrap and allow to infuse at room temperature for 3 hours or in a refrigerator overnight. If not using within 24 hours, chill in the refrigerator until ready to use.

5 **For Pesto Butter:** In a blender, combine ½ cup loosely packed fresh basil, ¼ cup grated Parmesan cheese, 2 tablespoons toasted pine nuts, 1 small clove minced garlic, ½ teaspoon lemon juice, ⅛ teaspoon salt, and ⅛ teaspoon pepper. Pulse until it has a texture like bread crumbs. Add 2 tablespoons olive oil and blend until smooth. In a bowl, stir together butter and contents of blender until smooth. If not using within 24 hours, cover and chill in the refrigerator until ready to use.

Fruit Curd

Makes 1 cup

Note that these curds (and the fruit syrups on page 246 and 248) call for frozen fruit. Since syrups and curds involve boiling the fruit and discarding the pulp, frozen fruit is a cost-effective alternative to fresh. However, if you have fresh berries you would like to use up before they spoil, you can. Fresh fruit yields approximately ¼ cup more curd.

INGREDIENTS

1 lb. frozen blackberries, blueberries, or raspberries
2 tablespoons fresh lemon juice
¼ cup sugar
2 tablespoons butter, softened
1 tablespoon cornstarch

Special Tools

1 (10-oz.) mason jar, sterilized
Wire-mesh strainer

INSTRUCTIONS

1 In a medium saucepan over medium-low heat, cook the berries, lemon juice, and 1 tablespoon water for 15 minutes, stirring occasionally, until berries are fully thawed and very soft. Strain the mixture, pressing the fruit through the strainer with a spoon. Scrape bottom of the strainer to be sure to get all the fruit pulp as well. Discard the waste left in the strainer. Return berry juice to pan and place over medium heat. Whisk in the sugar and butter until dissolved. Bring the mix to a boil, stirring occasionally. In a small bowl, whisk 1 tablespoon water and cornstarch into a slurry. Add the slurry to the berry mix and heat 3 minutes, stirring continuously. The mixture will thicken.

2 Transfer to a mason jar and cover the top tightly with plastic wrap, making sure the wrap doesn't touch the hot curd. Allow the curd to cool for 15 minutes on the counter. Remove plastic, screw on the lid, and chill in the refrigerator for 2 hours or until completely cool. Chill until ready to use.

Homemade Marshmallows

Makes 1 (8" x 8") pan

Homemade marshmallows are worlds better than store bought and easy to customize. Plain vanilla marshmallows cut into squares are an elegant gift, but it's also fun to play with flavors and cookie cutters. Check the note in the margin for instructions for gingerbread and mint versions of this recipe!

INGREDIENTS

¼ cup plus 2 tablespoons cold water

1½ tablespoons gelatin powder or 2 (0.25-oz.) packets

¼ cup room-temperature water

¼ cup plus 2 tablespoons corn syrup

¾ cup sugar

Pinch salt

1½ teaspoon vanilla extract

¼ cup cornstarch

¼ cup powdered sugar

Special Tools

Candy thermometer

*To make gingerbread marshmallows, simply replace the vanilla with ½ teaspoon ground ginger, ¼ teaspoon cinnamon, ¼ teaspoon allspice, and ⅛ teaspoon ground cloves. Cut marshmallows into mini gingerbread men using a 2½-inch cookie cutter.

**To make mint marshmallows, replace the vanilla with 1 teaspoon mint extract.

INSTRUCTIONS

1 Line an 8" x 8" baking pan with aluminum foil. Spray the foil with cooking spray and set aside.

2 Add ¼ cup and 2 tablespoons of cold water to the bowl of a standing mixer. Sprinkle in gelatin and stir gently to combine. Allow to bloom for 10 minutes.

3 While you wait, add ¼ cup room-temperature water, corn syrup, sugar, and salt to a medium saucepan. Do not stir. Heat on medium high until the mixture reaches 240 to 250°F (approximately 10 minutes), swirling the pan occasionally.

4 Turn the mixer on low for 30 seconds to break up the gelatin, then very slowly pour in the hot sugar mix, taking care not to touch the sides of the pan. Gradually increase the speed to the highest setting and beat until the mixture is white and opaque and the bowl is almost completely cool to the touch (approximately 10 minutes). Beat in the vanilla and any desired coloring until well combined.

5 Coat a spatula with cooking spray and very quickly scrape the marshmallow mixture into the foil-lined pan, spreading quickly until even.

6 Whisk together cornstarch and powdered sugar and sift a tablespoon over the marshmallow mixture. Cover loosely with plastic wrap and allow to set overnight.

7 Sift approximately ¼ cup of the cornstarch mix over a cutting board and overturn the set marshmallow onto the board. Coat a knife or the edge of a cookie cutter in cooking spray and cut out shapes.

8 Add to a bowl and toss in remaining cornstarch mix. To store, tap off excess cornstarch mixture and place in a large sealed plastic bag.

Honeycomb Candy

Makes 10 ounces

This unique, fragrant candy tastes great on its own and can also be crumbled and used as a garnish atop Pooh's Honey Lemon Cookies on page 127.

INGREDIENTS

¾ cup granulated sugar
½ cup honey
¼ cup corn syrup
½ teaspoon almond or
vanilla extract
⅛ teaspoon salt
1 teaspoon baking soda

Special Tools

Candy thermometer

INSTRUCTIONS

1 Line a 9" x 13" baking dish with parchment paper, making sure the edges of the paper extend at least 2 inches above the pan. Set aside.

2 Add the granulated sugar to the center of a medium saucepan. Pour the honey, corn syrup, extract, and salt over the sugar. Place over medium heat and bring to 300°F (do not stir). Remove from heat and add the baking soda all at once, whisking until well combined.*

3 Carefully pour the mixture into the prepared pan. If the parchment paper is not sitting firmly in the bottom of the pan, the mixture should weigh it down.

4 Allow to rest for 45 minutes until hard and completely cool.

5 Strike with a spoon to break into small pieces. Store in a sealed plastic bag.

*The baking soda causes a chemical reaction, making the hot sugar mix foam upward very quickly. Always use caution when working with hot sugar.

Infused Honey

Makes 6 ounces honey

More than just a sweetener, honey adds complexity to everything, from cocktails to glazes for poultry or fish. It also makes a wonderful condiment for bread or drizzling over cheese. Increase your honey's versatility by infusing it with fun flavors like lavender, cinnamon, and even bourbon! More uses are included in the instructions below.

INGREDIENTS

6 ounces honey

Special Tools

1 (8-oz.) mason jar and lid, sterilized

INSTRUCTIONS

1 For Bourbon Honey: Stir 2 tablespoons bourbon into honey until well combined. Pour into mason jar and seal.

- **Uses:** Baking, bread and cheese condiment, cocktails, poultry glaze

2 For Garlic and Herb Honey: To the mason jar add 1 large sprig fresh rosemary, 1 large sprig fresh thyme, and 3 cloves peeled garlic. Pour honey into jar. Make sure contents are completely submerged and tap jar lightly on the counter to dispel air bubbles. Seal tightly. Let sit for 1 week, periodically turning over the jar. Taste with a clean spoon after 1 week. If desired flavor level has been reached, remove and discard add-ins. If not, continue to taste every 2 to 3 days.

- **Uses:** Bread and cheese condiment, fish and poultry glaze, roasted vegetable glaze

3 For Floral Honey: To the mason jar add 1 teaspoon vanilla extract and 2 tablespoons food-grade lavender buds. Pour honey into jar and seal tightly. Let sit for 1 week, periodically turning over the jar. Taste with a clean spoon after 1 week. If desired flavor level has been reached, scoop out lavender with a slotted spoon and discard. If not, continue to taste every 2 to 3 days.

- **Uses:** Baking, beverage sweetener

4 For Spiced Honey: To the mason jar add 2 cinnamon sticks, 2 star anise seedpods, and $1/4$ teaspoon whole cloves. Pour honey into jar. Make sure contents are completely submerged and lightly tap jar on counter to dispel air bubbles. Seal tightly. Let sit for 1 week, periodically turning over the jar. Taste with a clean spoon after 1 week. If

(Continued on next page)

desired flavor level has been reached, remove and discard add-ins. If not, continue to taste every 2 to 3 days.

- **Uses:** Baking, beverage sweetener, bread and cheese condiment, oatmeal/pancake/waffle topper, cocktails, poultry glaze

5 For Lemon-Ginger-Mint Honey: To the mason jar add 1.5 ounces fresh ginger (peeled), 2 1″ x 2″ strips lemon peel, and 1 large sprig fresh mint. Pour honey into jar. Make sure contents are completely submerged and lightly tap jar on counter to dispel air bubbles. Seal tightly. Let sit for 1 week, periodically turning over the jar. Taste with a clean spoon after 1 week. If desired flavor level has been reached, remove and discard add-ins. If not, continue to taste every 2 to 3 days.

- **Uses:** Beverage sweetener, cocktails, poultry glaze

Infused Sugar

Makes ¾ cup sugar

Infused sugars make a unique sweetener in your favorite tea, substitute for plain sugar in baking recipes, or garnish on the rim of cocktail glasses.

INGREDIENTS

¾ cup sugar

Add-in Options

2 teaspoons Earl Grey tea (removed from bag), or

2 teaspoons chai tea (removed from bag), or

2 tablespoons food-grade lavender buds, or

1 tablespoon lemon/or lime/or orange zest, or

2 tablespoons finely crushed freeze-dried strawberries

Special Tools

1 (8-oz.) mason jar and lid, sterilized

INSTRUCTIONS

1   Combine the sugar and the option of your choice in a bowl and whisk until thoroughly combined. Transfer to mason jar and seal tightly. For citrus zest sugars, store in the refrigerator. Allow to infuse for at least 1 week before use, shaking the jar periodically.

Pesto

These pestos make a festively colored Christmas gift when paired together. The basil pesto can also be gifted at a Wizard of Oz party at Halloween as "melted witch pesto"!

Basil Pesto

Makes ½ cup

INGREDIENTS

1 cup fresh basil,
loosely packed
½ cup grated
Parmesan cheese
¼ cup pine nuts, toasted
(to toast, place on a
baking sheet in a 325°F
oven for 3–5 minutes.)
2 small cloves garlic,
minced
1 teaspoon lemon juice
¼ teaspoon salt
¼ teaspoon pepper
6 tablespoons olive oil

INSTRUCTIONS

1 Add all the ingredients except the olive oil to a food processor and process on low until the mixture is well combined and has a grainy consistency. Gradually add in the olive oil and process until combined.

Sun-Dried Tomato Pesto

Makes a little over 1 cup

INGREDIENTS

8 ounces sun-dried tomatoes packed in olive oil

½ cup Parmesan cheese

¼ cup pine nuts, toasted (to toast, place on a baking sheet in a 325°F oven for 3–5 minutes.)

1 teaspoon lemon juice

1 clove garlic

¼ teaspoon salt

¼ teaspoon pepper

INSTRUCTIONS

1 Separate tomatoes from oil and set oil aside. Process tomatoes and all other ingredients together in a food processor on low speed until mixture forms a paste. Add ¼ cup reserved oil and process until combined. If making for use in the Pizza Pinwheel Cyclones on page 171, end here (some oil is left out for use in that recipe to avoid leaks while baking). If making the pesto on its own, continue to add reserved oil until the mixture reaches the texture of a thick sauce.

Syrups

Homemade syrups make a lovely gift because they keep for ages, and it's easy to make a big batch to give to everyone on your gift list.

Blueberry Syrup

Makes 1¼ cups

INGREDIENTS

1 lb. frozen blueberries
1 cup water
½ cup sugar

Special Tools

Wire-mesh strainer

INSTRUCTIONS

1 Add all ingredients to a medium-sized pot and bring to a boil on medium-high heat, stirring until the sugar is dissolved. Reduce heat to medium-low, cover, and allow to simmer for 10 minutes. Strain the liquid into a bowl (do not press down on the berries to release extra juice). Discard berries.

2 Return the liquid to the pot and bring back to a boil on medium-high heat. Reduce heat to medium-low again and heat for 10 minutes, uncovered, stirring occasionally. The mixture will thicken somewhat. Transfer liquid to a sealable container. Cover and chill in the refrigerator until ready to use. The mixture will thicken slightly more after it cools.

Pumpkin Syrup

Makes 2¼ cups

INGREDIENTS

7.5 ounces
  pumpkin puree
2 cups water
½ cup brown sugar,
  packed
½ cup granulated sugar
1 teaspoon cinnamon
½ teaspoon nutmeg
¼ teaspoon cloves
¼ teaspoon ginger

Special Tools

Wire-mesh strainer

INSTRUCTIONS

1 Combine all ingredients in a medium saucepan over medium-high heat and whisk until smooth. Bring to boiling. Reduce heat to medium-low and simmer for 10 minutes, whisking regularly.

2 Pass mixture through a wire-mesh strainer 3 times, discarding the deposits in the strainer between straining. Transfer liquid to a sealable container. Cover and chill in the refrigerator until ready to use.*

Strawberry Syrup

Makes 1½ cups

INGREDIENTS

1 lb. frozen strawberries
1 cup water
½ cup sugar

Special Tools

Wire-mesh strainer

INSTRUCTIONS

1 Add all ingredients to a medium-sized pot and bring to a boil on medium-high heat, stirring until the sugar is dissolved. Reduce heat to medium-low, cover, and allow to simmer for 10 minutes. Strain the liquid from the strawberries into a bowl (do not press down on the berries to release extra juice).

2 Return the liquid to the pot and bring back to a boil on medium-high heat. Reduce heat to medium-low again and heat for 10 minutes, uncovered, stirring occasionally. The mixture will thicken. Transfer liquid to a sealable container. Cover and chill in the refrigerator until ready to use. The mixture will thicken slightly more as it cools.

*Because the pumpkin syrup contains real pumpkin puree instead of just pumpkin pie spice flavoring, expect a small amount of separation to occur between the sugar syrup and pumpkin solids as the material settles. This has no effect on flavor, but if giving this syrup as a gift, you may want to package it in an opaque or colored glass bottle for best visual appeal.

Note: Frozen fruit is a cost-effective alternative to fresh fruit in syrups, but you can absolutely use fresh if you want. Just substitute out an equal amount of fresh for frozen fruit and increase the water by ½ cup. It will yield about ½ cup more syrup.

Note: You may notice that the syrup recipes in this book warn against pressing the fruit while straining, while the curd recipes say to do just that. This is because pressing the fruit allows bits of skin and pulp into the strained liquid. For syrups, this can make the final product cloudy and unappetizing. This isn't an issue for curds, which are already opaque due to the addition of thickeners like cornstarch or egg.

References

Alcott, Louisa M. *Little Women*. New York: Puffin Books, 2014.

Andersen, Hans C. "The Snow Queen: An Adventure in Seven Stories." *Fairy Tales*. Translated by Marte Hvam Hulte. New York: Barnes & Noble, 2007.

Baum, L. Frank. *The Wonderful Wizard of Oz*. Luton: Andrews UK Ltd, 2012.

Carroll, Lewis. *Alice's Adventures in Wonderland & Through the Looking-Glass*. Millennium Publications, 2014.

Dickens, Charles. *A Christmas Carol*. New York: Bantam Books, 1986.

Doyle, Arthur C. "The Adventure of the Beryl Coronet." *The Complete Sherlock Holmes*. Vol. I. New York: Barnes & Noble, 2003.

Doyle, Arthur C. "The Adventure of the Engineer's Thumb." *The Complete Sherlock Holmes*. Vol. I. New York: Barnes & Noble, 2003.

Doyle, Arthur C. "The Five Orange Pips." *The Complete Sherlock Holmes*. Vol. I. New York: Barnes & Noble, 2003.

Doyle, Arthur C. "The Sign of the Four." *The Complete Sherlock Holmes*. Vol. I. New York: Barnes & Noble, 2003.

Doyle, Arthur C. "The Valley of Fear." *The Complete Sherlock Holmes*. Vol. II. New York: Barnes & Noble, 2003.

Hoffman, E. T. A., and Maurice Sendak. *Nutcracker*. Translated by Ralph Manheim. New York: Crown Publishers, 1984.

Irving, Washington. *The Legend of Sleepy Hollow and Other Writings*. New York: Sterling, 2005.

Jacques, Brian. *The Legend of Luke*. New York: Ace Books, 2001.

Jacques, Brian. *Loamhedge*. Illustrated by David Elliot. New York: Firebird, 2003.

Jacques, Brian, and Sean Rubin. *The Rogue Crew*. New York: Philomel Books, 2011.

Jacques, Brian, and David Elliot. *Doomwyte*. New York: Philomel, 2008.

Leroux, Gaston, Mireille Ribiere, and Jann Matlock. *The Phantom of the Opera*. London: Penguin Books, 2012.

Lewis, C. S., and Pauline Baynes. *The Lion, the Witch, and the Wardrobe*. New York: HarperCollins, 1994.

Lewis, C. S., and Pauline Baynes. *The Magician's Nephew*. New York: HarperCollins, 1994.

Lewis, C. S., and Pauline Baynes. *The Voyage of the* Dawn Treader. New York: HarperCollins, 1994.

London, Jack. *White Fang*. New York: Dover Publications, 1991.

Milne, A. A., and Ernest H. Shepard. *The House at Pooh Corner*. New York: Puffin Books, 1992.

Milne, A. A., and Ernest H. Shepard. *Winnie-the-Pooh*. New York: Dutton Children's Books, 1988.

Poe, Edgar A. "The Fall of the House of Usher." *Complete Tales and Poems*. New York: Fall River, 2012.

Poe, Edgar A. "The Premature Burial." *Complete Tales and Poems*. New York: Fall River, 2012.

Poe, Edgar A. "The Masque of the Red Death." *Complete Tales and Poems*. New York: Fall River, 2012.

Poe, Edgar A. "The Raven." *Complete Tales and Poems*. New York: Fall River, 2012.

Stoker, Bram. *Dracula*. New York: Barnes & Noble, 2003.

Tolkien, J. R. R. *The Hobbit, or, There and Back Again*. Boston: Mariner Books, Houghton Mifflin Harcourt, 2012.

Wilder, Laura Ingalls. *Little House in the Big Woods*. Full Color ed. New York: HarperCollins, 2004.

Wilder, Laura Ingalls. *Little House on the Prairie*. Full Color ed. New York: HarperCollins, 2004.

Conversion Charts

METRIC AND IMPERIAL CONVERSIONS

(These conversions are rounded for convenience)

Ingredient	Cups/Tablespoons/ Teaspoons	Ounces	Grams/Milliliters
Butter	1 cup/ 16 tablespoons/ 2 sticks	8 ounces	230 grams
Cheese, shredded	1 cup	4 ounces	110 grams
Cream cheese	1 tablespoon	0.5 ounce	14.5 grams
Cornstarch	1 tablespoon	0.3 ounce	8 grams
Flour, all-purpose	1 cup/1 tablespoon	4.5 ounces/0.3 ounce	125 grams/8 grams
Flour, whole wheat	1 cup	4 ounces	120 grams
Fruit, dried	1 cup	4 ounces	120 grams
Fruits or veggies, chopped	1 cup	5 to 7 ounces	145 to 200 grams
Fruits or veggies, pureed	1 cup	8.5 ounces	245 grams
Honey, maple syrup, or corn syrup	1 tablespoon	0.75 ounce	20 grams
Liquids: cream, milk, water, or juice	1 cup	8 fluid ounces	240 milliliters
Oats	1 cup	5.5 ounces	150 grams
Salt	1 teaspoon	0.2 ounce	6 grams
Spices: cinnamon, cloves, ginger, or nutmeg (ground)	1 teaspoon	0.2 ounce	5 milliliters
Sugar, brown, firmly packed	1 cup	7 ounces	200 grams
Sugar, white	1 cup/1 tablespoon	7 ounces/0.5 ounce	200 grams/12.5 grams
Vanilla extract	1 teaspoon	0.2 ounce	4 grams

OVEN TEMPERATURES

Fahrenheit	Celsius	Gas Mark
225°	110°	$\frac{1}{4}$
250°	120°	$\frac{1}{2}$
275°	140°	1
300°	150°	2
325°	160°	3
350°	180°	4
375°	190°	5
400°	200°	6
425°	220°	7
450°	230°	8

Index

A

Alice's Adventures in Wonderland, 177, 179, 221

almonds
   Garlic Rosemary Toasted Almonds, 49
   Mirror Shard Mini Ice Cream Cakes, 217

amaretto
   Mirror Shard Mini Ice Cream Cakes, 217

apples
   Applesauce, 13
   Apple Cider Crullers, 109
   Apple Rose Tartlets, 197–198
   Bag End Orchard Salad, 83
   Baked Apples, 43
   Maple Walnut Apple Pie, 115

Arctic Trail Coffee Muffins, 61

B

bacon
   Devils on Horseback, 195
   Fried Snowballs, 209–210
   Pesto and Bacon Puff Pastry Christmas Tree, 51–53
   White Whiskey Baked Beans with Bacon, 65

Bag End Orchard Salad, 83

baked Alaska
   S'mores Baked Alaska, 67–68

baked apples, 43

bananas
   Beorn's Honey Nut Banana Bread, 75

Basil Pesto, 244

beans
   White Whiskey Baked Beans with Bacon, 65

beef
   Robber "Stakes", 135
   Sherlock's Steak Sandwiches, 161

beets
   Deeper 'n Ever Turnip 'n Tater 'n Beetroot Pie, 101–102
   Rabbit's Autumn Harvest Salad, 125

Beorn's Honey Nut Banana Bread, 75

bitters
   Phantom's Rose, The, 225
   Poe's Nevermore Cocktail, 227

blackberry
   Blackberry Curd, 238
   Blackberry Sauce, 27

Blood Orange Scones, 155–156

blueberries
   Blueberry Curd, 238
   Blueberry Syrup, 246
   Poe's Nevermore Cocktail, 227

bread
   Beorn's Honey Nut Banana Bread, 75
   Dracula's Dinner Rolls, 137–138
   Loamhedge Nutbread, 97
   Rustic Whole Wheat Bread, 37–38
   Savory Snowflake Bread, 211–213
   Skillet Cornbread with Homemade Butter, 87–88

Brown Sugar Glazed Turkey, 111

butter
   Flavored Butter, 237

C

Candied Walnuts, 236

caramelized onions
   Savory Snowflake Bread, 211–213

Camembert
   Gerda's Cherry Bites, 215

Curd Suit Cheese Bites, 181–182

carrots
   Cottleston Pie, 123
   Deeper 'n Ever Turnip 'n Tater 'n Beetroot Pie, 101–102
   Rabbit's Autumn Harvest Salad, 125

cheddar
  Mouse King Cheese Bites, 55
cheese
  Camembert
    Gerda's Cherry Bites, 215
  cheddar
    Mouse King Cheese Bites, 55
  goat
    Bag End Orchard Salad, 83
    Diggory's Apple Bites, 25
    Queen of Hearts's Tomato Tart,
      The, 183–185
  Gouda
    Apple Rose Tartlets, 197–198
  Gruyère
    Savory Snowflake Bread, 211–213
  Parmesan
    Basil Pesto, 244
    Leek and Potato Soup with Parsnip
      and Garlic, 99
    Sun-Dried Tomato Pesto, 245
  ricotta
    Savory Strawberry Éclairs, 199
cherries
  Gerda's Cherry Bites, 215
  Sugar Plums, 57
chicken
  Cottleston Pie, 123
chips
  Melted Witch Chips and Guacamole,
    173
  Rabbit's Autumn Harvest Salad, 125
  Renfield's Spider Chips and Salsa,
    133
chocolate
  Chocolate Profiterole Christmas
    Puddings, 17
  Chocolate Strawberry Opera Cake,
    203
  Hobbit Door Giant Chocolate Chip
    Cookie, 79–81
Christmas, 9, 11, 35, 51

Christmas Carol, A, 9, 11
Chronicles of Narnia, The, 23
coffee
  Arctic Trail Coffee Muffins, 61
Coffin Pizza Pockets, 147
cornbread
  Skillet Cornbread with Homemade
    Butter, 87–88
Cottleston Pie, 123
cranberries
  Turkey Roulade, 39–41
cupcakes
  Eat Me Cakes, 189–190
  Mirror Shard Mini Ice Cream Cakes,
    217
Curd, Fruit, 238

D
Damson Plum and Pear Crumbles with
  Meadowcream and Mint, 103–105
dates
  Devils on Horseback, 195
  Sugar Plums, 57
Deeper 'n Ever Turnip 'n Tater 'n
  Beetroot Pie, 101–102
deer
  Venison Pot Roast, 91
Deviled Raven Eggs, 145
Devils on Horseback, 195
Diggory's Apple Bites, 25
dill
  Seared Salmon with Lemon Dill
    Butter, 63
Dracula, 129, 131
Dracula's Dinner Rolls, 137–138
Drink Me Punch, 221
Duchess Potatoes, 21

E
Eat Me Cakes, 189–190
Éclairs, Savory Strawberry, 199
eggs
  Deviled Raven Eggs, 145

Roasted Tomato Deviled Scotch
    Eggs, 157–159
Emerald City Popcorn, 169

F
figs
    Savory Snowflake Bread, 211–213
    Sugar Plums, 57
Flavored Butter, 237
food gifts, 235
Fried Snowballs, 209–210
frosting
    buttercream, 189, 190
    cream cheese, 189, 190
    Earl Grey, 163
Fruit Curd, 238

G
ganache
    Chocolate Strawberry Opera Cake,
        203
garlic
    Garlic Rosemary Toasted Almonds,
        49
    Roasted Garlic, 97
gelatin
    Card Suit Cheese Bites, 181–182
Gerda's Cherry Bites, 215
gingerbread
    Jo's Gingerbread, 44–45
    Jo March's Hot Cocoa Mix, 223
ginger ale
    Wicked Witch Punch, 233
goat cheese
    Bag End Orchard Salad, 83
    Diggory's Apple Bites, 25
    Queen of Hearts's Tomato Tart, The,
        183–185
Goose, Onion and Sage Roasted, 15–16
Gouda
    Apple Rose Tartlets, 197–198
Gruyère
    Savory Snowflake Bread, 211–213

guacamole
    Melted Witch Chips and Guacamole,
        173

H
Halloween, 129, 135, 219, 227, 244
Haycorns, 121
Herbed Mushroom Puffs, 187
Hobbit Door Giant Chocolate Chip
    Cookie, 79–81
Hobbit, The, 71, 73
hot cocoa
    Jo March's Hot Cocoa Mix, 223
    White Witch's White Chocolate Chai
        Latte, 231
hot water crust
    Melton Mowbray: Mini Pork Pies,
        77–78
Homemade Marshmallows, 239
honey
    Beorn's Honey Nut Banana Bread, 75
    Diggory's Apple Bites, 25
    Infused Honey, 241–242
    Honeycomb Candy, 240
    Pooh's Honey Lemon Cookies, 127
horseradish
    Sherlock's Steak Sandwiches, 161

I
ice cream
    Mirror Shard Mini Ice Cream
        Cupcakes, 217
infused
    Infused Honey, 241–242
    Infused Sugar, 243

J
Jo's Gingerbread, 44–45
Jo March's Hot Cocoa Mix, 223

K
kale
    Bag End Orchard Salad, 83

kiwi fruit
    Wicked Witch Punch, 233

L
lavender buds
    Infused Honey, 241–242
    Infused Sugar, 243
Leek and Potato Soup with Parsnip and
    Garlic, 99
lemonade
    Drink Me Punch, 221
Little Women, 9, 35, 223
Little House on the Prairie, 85, 87, 89, 91
Loamhedge Nutbread, 97
London Fog Mystery Cookies, 163–164

M
maple
    Maple Candy, 93
    Maple Walnut Apple Pie, 115
Marshmallows, Homemade, 239
Masque of the Red Death Skeleton
    Cookies, 151
mayonnaise
    Roasted Tomato Deviled Scotch
      Eggs, 157–159
Melted Witch Chips and Guacamole,
    173
Melton Mowbray: Mini Pork Pies, 77–78
meringue
    S'mores Baked Alaska, 67–68
Mirror Shard Mini Ice Cream Cakes, 217
Monstrous Moon Pies, 139–141
Moon Phase Fries, 149
Mouse King Cheese Bites, 55
Mrs. Beaver's Potatoes, 33
mushrooms
    Herbed Mushroom Puffs, 187

N
Nutcracker, The, **47**
nuts
    almonds

Garlic Rosemary Toasted Almonds,
    49
Mirror Shard Mini Ice Cream
      Cupcakes, 217
pine nuts
    Bag End Orchard Salad, 83
    Spiced Pine Nuts, 236
pistachios
    Sugar Plums, 57
walnuts
    Loamhedge Nutbread, 97

O
Onion and Sage Roasted Goose, 15–16
oranges
    Blood Orange Scones, 155–156

P
Parmesan
    Basil Pesto, 244
    Leek and Potato Soup with Parsnip
      and Garlic, 99
    Sun-Dried Tomato Pesto, 245
parsnip
    Leek and Potato Soup with Parsnip
      and Garlic, 99
pears
    Bag End Orchard Salad, 83
    Damson Plum and Pear Crumbles
      with Meadowcream and Mint,
      103–105
    Turkey Roulade, 39–41
pecans
    Damson Plum and Pear Crumbles
      with Meadowcream and Mint,
      103–105
pesto
    Basil Pesto, 244
    Pesto and Bacon Puff Pastry
      Christmas Tree, 51–53
    Sun-Dried Tomato Pesto, 245
Phantom of the Opera, The, 177, 193, 225
Phantom's Rose, The, 225

pine nuts
    Bag End Orchard Salad, 83
    Spiced Pine Nuts, 236
pistachios
    Sugar Plums, 57
pizza
    Coffin Pizza Pockets, 147
    Pizza Pinwheel Cyclones, 171
Poe, Edgar Allan, 129, 143, 227
Poe's Nevermore Cocktail, 227
Pooh's Honey Lemon Cookies, 127
pomegranate
    Bag End Orchard Salad, 83
    Diggory's Apple Bites, 25
    Drink Me Punch, 221
popcorn
    Emerald City Popcorn, 169
pork
    Melton Mowbray: Mini Pork Pies,
      17–18
potatoes
    Cottleston Pie, 123
    Deeper 'n Ever Turnip 'n Tater 'n
      Beetroot Pie, 101–102
    Duchess Potatoes, 21
    Fried Snowballs, 209–210
    Leek and Potato Soup with Parsnip
      and Garlic, 99
    Moon Phase Fries, 149
    Mrs. Beaver's Potatoes, 33
    Rabbit's Autumn Harvest Salad, 125
    Simple Roasted Sweet Potatoes, 89
Profiterole, Chocolate Christmas
    Pudding, 17
prunes
    Sugar Plums, 57
Pudding, Chocolate Profiterole
    Christmas, 17
pumpkin
    Pumpkin Cider, 229
    Pumpkin Syrup, 247
    Pumpkin Winged Monkey Bread, 175

    Smashed Pumpkin Soup, 113

Q
Queen of Hearts's Tomato Tart, The,
    183–185

R
Rabbit's Autumn Harvest Salad, 125
Raspberry Curd, 238
Redwall, 71, 95
Renfield's Spider Chips and Salsa, 133
ricotta
    Queen of Hearts's Tomato Tart, The,
      183–185
    Savory Strawberry Éclairs, 199
roasted garlic, 97
Roasted Tomato Deviled Scotch Eggs,
    157–159
Robber "Stakes", 135
rum
    Sugar Plums, 57
Rustic Whole Wheat Bread, 37–38

S
S'mores Baked Alaska, 67–68
Savory Snowflake Bread, 211–213
Savory Strawberry Éclairs, 199
Seared Salmon with Lemon Dill Butter,
    63
Scotch eggs
    Roasted Tomato Deviled Scotch
      Eggs, 157–159
Sherlock Holmes, 153, 155, 161
Sherlock's Steak Sandwiches, 161
Simple Roasted Sweet Potatoes, 89
Skillet Cornbread with Homemade
    Butter, 87–88
Sleepy Hollow, The Legend of, 107, 229
Smashed Pumpkin Soup, 113
Snow Queen, The, 177, 207
Spiced Pine Nuts, 236
squash
    butternut, 101

steak
  Robber "Stakes", 135
  Sherlock's Steak Sandwiches, 161
strawberries
  Chocolate Strawberry Opera Cake,
    203
  Savory Strawberry Éclairs, 199
  Strawberry Syrup, 248
Sugar, Infused, 243
Sugar Plums, 57
Sun-Dried Tomato Pesto, 245
sweet potatoes
  Simple Roasted Sweet Potatoes, 89
syrup, 246–248

T
tea
  Card Suit Cheese Bites, 181–182
Thanksgiving, 71, 73, 87, 93, 101, 113, 123,
  229
tomatoes
  Queen of Hearts's Tomato Tart, The,
    183–185
  Roasted Tomato Deviled Scotch
    Eggs, 157–159
turkey
  Brown Sugar Glazed Turkey, 111
  Turkey from Aslan's Table, 27–28
  Turkey Roulade, 39–41

Turkish Delight, 29–31
turnips
  Deeper 'n Ever Turnip 'n Tater 'n
    Beetroot Pie, 101–102

V
Venison Pot Roast, 91
vinegar
  Strawberry Balsamic, 199

W
walnuts
  Loamhedge Nutbread, 97
Wicked Witch Punch, 233
Winnie-the-Pooh, 119, 121, 123, 127
White Fang, 59
White Whiskey Baked Beans with
  Bacon, 65
White Witch's White Chocolate Chai
  Latte, 231
whiskey
  White Whiskey Baked Beans with
    Bacon, 65
wine
  Drink Me Punch, 221
  Phantom's Rose, The, 225
  Poe's Nevermore Cocktail, 227
Wonderful Wizard of Oz, The, 167, 233